# What Other

*Ying and Grace Kai's Training for Trainers* offers us a brilliantly simple, expertly proven and thoroughly biblical approach to advancing the Jesus mission. This is exactly the kind of text that every church planter should read. Ying & Grace Kai have been used by God to do what so many of us dream of and they describe how in this terrific new book!

Dave Ferguson
Lead Pastor - Community Christian Church
Lead Visionary - NewThing

*Ying and Grace Kai's Training for Trainers* provides the most reliable resource available today for catalyzing Church Planting Movements. With personal insights and stories from around the world, this book pulls back the curtain and shows you the lives and life lessons behind the movements that have changed the world.

Dr. David Garrison
Missionary author
*Church Planting Movements*

In this era of multiplying church planting movements, few methodological approaches have had more impact than T4T in its many cultural adaptations around the world. T4T has provided sails that ordinary believers can raise to move with the winds of the Spirit. More than the method, however, are the man and woman. As movements are more caught than taught, the Kais have humbly modeled the sacrificial spirit of faith needed to see God move in power and inspired tens of thousands. I heartily commend this account of how God has used them.

Dr. Steve Smith
Author and Trainer
*T4T: A Discipleship Re-Revolution*

I've been a student of movements that multiply disciples and churches for thirty years. Ying and Grace Kai are standouts as pioneers, catalysts, trainers and strategists for church planting movements.

To meet them is to be infected by their contagious love for Jesus and their passion to reach people far from God. This book is a treasure trove of case studies, principles and practices for people who share their heart for God and the Great Commission.

Steve Addison
Author of *Pioneering Movements*

From 2000 – 2007 I was Ying and Grace Kai's agency supervisor when amazing multiplication of disciples began. My wife and I traveled with them, interviewed new believers and trainers, tabulated numbers, and verified miraculous stories from the original T4T movement. The assessment team I later led spent weeks interviewing, verifying numerical results, and seeing spiritual transformation. A godly man and woman leading a holy life, with a passion for lostness; to God be the glory.

Dr. Bill Smith
Trainer and Missionary Emeritus, International Mission Board, SBC

A friend who had just heard about T4T, asked if this was just another 'fad' in church outreach. I wish I would have had this book to give him then. This book not only revisits the amazing core principles that are at the heart of church-planting movements around the world, but looks at the bigger picture of how multiplying movements of disciples can be built in existing churches, Western contexts, and places where 'we have just always done it that way.'

Dennis Sink
Global Church Movements, CCCI

*Ying and Grace Kai's Training for Trainers* has arrived at last! It puts into one precious volume the principles that have become legendary over the last decade among those of us who have looked to them for guidance about how to help everyone, everywhere experience God's love through Jesus Christ. Their book tells us what we already knew: T4T is not primarily a method or a set of techniques, it is a whole-hearted lifestyle, a way of living with Jesus in the power of his Holy Spirit. The Kais provide a practical answer to the most important questions every follower of Jesus must ask: How can I live like Jesus, and how can I teach others to live like Jesus in such a way that they can teach others to live like Jesus.

Erick Schenkel
Executive Director
Jesus Film Project

Ying and Grace Kai's
Training for Trainers

*Ying and Grace Kai's*

# TRAINING FOR TRAINERS
The Movement that Changed the World

## by Ying and Grace Kai

**WIGTake Resources**
P.O. Box 1884, Monument, CO 80132
www.WIGTakeResources.org
Product Distribution: NoHutch@wigtake.org

ISBN: 978-1-939124-12-8

1. Missions. 2. Evangelism.
Kai, Ying, 1949 –
Kai, Grace, 1952 –

Printed by Bookmasters
Cover Design by Mike Mirabella
Interior Design by Megan Chadwick
Websites: www.T4TOnline.org
www.WIGTake.org
www.ChurchPlantingMovements.com/bookstore

Kai, Ying and Grace
   Ying and Grace Kai's Training for Trainers

# Table of Contents

Foreword . . . . . . . . . . . . . . . . . . . . . . . . . . . . . . . . . . . . . . . . . . vii

**PART ONE: FOUNDATIONS OF T4T**
1. Our Testimony . . . . . . . . . . . . . . . . . . . . . . . . . . . . . . . 3
2. The Heavenly Father's Heart . . . . . . . . . . . . . . . . . . . . 21
3. The Kingdom Worker. . . . . . . . . . . . . . . . . . . . . . . . . . 25
4. The Power of the Holy Spirit. . . . . . . . . . . . . . . . . . . . 35
5. The Joy of the Christian Life . . . . . . . . . . . . . . . . . . . . 57
6. The Power of Simplicity. . . . . . . . . . . . . . . . . . . . . . . . 61
7. Seven-Lesson Discipleship . . . . . . . . . . . . . . . . . . . . . 65
8. The T4T Process . . . . . . . . . . . . . . . . . . . . . . . . . . . . . 71
9. Hidden Wisdom . . . . . . . . . . . . . . . . . . . . . . . . . . . . . 79
10. T4T Testimonies . . . . . . . . . . . . . . . . . . . . . . . . . . . . . 85

**PART TWO: STABILIZING AND EXTENDING**
11. Building a Healthy Movement . . . . . . . . . . . . . . . . . . . 99
12. The Mid-Level Retreat . . . . . . . . . . . . . . . . . . . . . . . . 107
13. The Word and Prayer. . . . . . . . . . . . . . . . . . . . . . . . . 115
14. Forward Together. . . . . . . . . . . . . . . . . . . . . . . . . . . . 123
15. T4T in America . . . . . . . . . . . . . . . . . . . . . . . . . . . . . 129

**PART THREE: MATURING MOVEMENTS**
16. T4T in Existing Churches. . . . . . . . . . . . . . . . . . . . . . 147
17. Big Trainers. . . . . . . . . . . . . . . . . . . . . . . . . . . . . . . . 153
18. Words of Encouragement . . . . . . . . . . . . . . . . . . . . . 157

**APPENDIX A: T4T TRAINING LESSONS**
Lesson 1: The Assurance of Salvation . . . . . . . . . . . . . . . . 173
Lesson 2: Understanding Prayer . . . . . . . . . . . . . . . . . . . . 177
Lesson 3: Daily Devotions. . . . . . . . . . . . . . . . . . . . . . . . . 181
Lesson 4: The Church Gathering . . . . . . . . . . . . . . . . . . . . 185
Lesson 5: God is Our Heavenly Father . . . . . . . . . . . . . . . . 189
Lesson 6: Spreading the Gospel . . . . . . . . . . . . . . . . . . . . 193
Lesson 7: Participatory Bible Study. . . . . . . . . . . . . . . . . . 197

**APPENDIX B: BASIC T4T BIBLE STUDY PLAN**
Basic Bible Study Plan. . . . . . . . . . . . . . . . . . . . . . . . . . . 203
About the Authors . . . . . . . . . . . . . . . . . . . . . . . . . . . . . . 207
Acknowledgements . . . . . . . . . . . . . . . . . . . . . . . . . . . . . 209

# Foreword

If you knew there was someone God had used to bring two million souls to salvation in Jesus Christ, new believers who were baptized into 150,000 new churches in 10 years time, wouldn't you want to know more? I know I did. This is what drew me to Ying and Grace Kai whose Training for Trainers (T4T) movement in the first decade of the 21st century exploded into the largest and fastest growing Church Planting Movement we've ever seen.

I have been a student of Church Planting Movements for more than two decades. I've seen them in a variety of forms in many different religious, cultural, and linguistic settings, but I've never seen anything like T4T. Training for Trainers is something special, something that has earned the designation: *best practice*. Not only has T4T given us biblically faithful tools that produce new believers and disciples, it has proven to be transferable into myriad other cultures and languages, stimulating new movements all over the world.

After participating in Ying's Training for Trainers in 2004, my colleagues and I decided to see if it might work in South Asia where we were serving as missionaries. Over the next two years, our little house church used T4T to bring more than a thousand lost souls from seven different unreached people groups to faith and baptism, worshipping God in 106 new church starts. Others used T4T to produce an even greater harvest.

T4T is more than just a stand-alone process for multiplying disciples – though it does that quite well. I have also seen T4T woven into other strategies to transform them from good to great, from incremental to exponential, from courageous works to multiplying movements. Over the past decade, T4T has energized approaches such as the Jesus Film, disaster relief ministries, student ministries, Muslim ministries, and even the witness of traditional Protestant churches, catalyzing them to produce an exponential harvest of new believers and new churches filled with disciples who are doers of the Word and not passive hearers only.

This is why I was so excited to hear that Ying and Grace had written down the lessons they learned in their own movement and across a lifetime. They have shared these lessons with count-less missionaries and church planters, and now they are offering their story to the world. Ying wrote the initial draft of this book in Chinese, and though it has been translated into English, we have endeavored to keep Ying and Grace's own words as faithfully as possible. My prayer is that you will benefit from T4T's biblical tools, and perhaps more importantly, deepen your own walk with Christ as you absorb the life lessons from these servants of God.

David Garrison, Editor
*Ying and Grace Kai's Training for Trainers*

# PART ONE

*Foundations of T4T*

# 1

## Our Testimony

The coming of the Lord is near. How much time do we have left to spread the gospel to the ends of the earth? Today the world has a population of more than seven billion, but Christians only make up about one-third of that population. In Asia the Christian population is less than five percent. Even in much of Europe and the United States, many Christians are Christians in name only.

Many people attend Sunday worship as a formality, but how many are true disciples? Perhaps just a pitiful number. Therefore, we should rise up and proclaim the gospel; lead people to the Lord, and immediately train them to become disciples of the Lord. But this is more than a slogan, and more than just a program to spread the gospel.

We must obey the call, the mission, and the strategy of the Lord. This is so that the power and wisdom of the Holy Spirit will rapidly spread the gospel, as new believers, filled with the Holy Spirit, immediately train others to obey the Great Commission, and to share the gospel.

We are here to put the Lord's mission and call into every believer's heart and to understand the Father's will. To work according to his will, to train ourselves while guarding our hearts and minds. Then, by the wisdom and power given to us by the Holy Spirit, to urgently spread the gospel to everyone, and immediately train them to become disciples of the Lord.

Over the years we tried many different ways of discipleship training with limited fruitfulness. Since then we have learned that when Jesus gave us the mission to spread the gospel, he also gave us the best strategy for evangelism and the ability to practice that mission!

## OUR STORY

My wife Grace and I were missionaries in Asia for 21 years with the International Mission Board (IMB) of the Southern Baptist Convention. After a year of studying Cantonese, we began our church-planting ministry in Hong Kong. In those days, we still used a very traditional method of evangelism.

Each year, the two of us were able to lead 40 to 60 people to faith in Christ and start one new church. We thought we weren't doing too bad. At that time, our mission organization had given each missionary a guideline: each missionary should start at least one new church every five years, or they should transfer to another region since they were falling short of the East Asia region's standards. In our annual report each year we were able to report dozens of people coming to faith in Christ and the starting of a new church, so we thought we were doing pretty well.

We continued our service in Hong Kong until the year 2000. Then, after a stateside assignment in the United States, the Holy Spirit led us to shift our ministry to a large neighboring Asian country. Before that time, it had never occurred to us to serve in that country. In fact, we were afraid to go to a new place. After a time of sincere prayer, we made the decision to obey his calling. So we contacted our mission agency and requested a transfer of our ministry assignment.

In October of 2000, we were sent to Singapore for one month to participate in Strategy Coordinator (SC) training. A Strategy Coordinator is a missionary who develops and implements a strategy to reach an entire people group or population with the gospel of Jesus Christ.

On the first day of training, our training director asked each missionary unit to prepare a three-year master plan (mission strategy plan) and set an end vision within the three-year time frame. I did not understand what they meant by end vision, so I asked the training director, "What does end vision mean?" He responded, "Ying, it is very simple: how many people can you lead to Christ in the next three years and how many churches can you start?"

After hearing his explanation, Grace and I discussed how in three years, we had barely been able to bring less than 200 people to Christ and had only started three churches. As we studied the new region that the Lord was leading us to, we learned there were three cities in the area each of which had a registered population of 5.8 million. But then, we discovered that there were more than 15 million temporary factory workers from all over the country

## The Restaurant Owner

A restaurant owner from Taide traveled to attend one of our T4T trainings. He was a studious learner, had a heart for the people, and fear for the Lord. When he learned how to share the gospel, he listed all those around him he could train.

After returning to Taide, he faithfully trained every person on his name list. After a year, the number of new believers from the people he trained and the ones that were trained by those he trained already numbered more than a thousand.

The owner returned to his trainer and asked, "What is the next step? What do I do next?" At this time, we taught him how to start his Mid-Level Training Retreats. This would help encourage his trainers and allow them to spread the gospel even further.

After providing the retreat event, within a year, they were able to set up six other larger training camps. At each of these training camps, they were able to lead more than a thousand people to believe in Jesus. Thank the Lord for the restaurant owner in Taide who brought revival in two years. More than 6,000 were led to Jesus Christ!

Praise God!

that had come to these three cities to work in the thousands of factories! So there were actually more than 20 million people in our new mission assignment.

This was a lot of people! We thought to ourselves, if we were only able to lead around 200 people to Christ and start only three churches in three years, this number was so pitifully low. Even if we worked very hard to lead 1,000 believers and started 10 churches, the number was still too small for a population of 20 million. So we prayed and studied the Bible diligently every day, asking the Father to give us the best strategy to share the gospel.

I remember when our training director challenged us to find more than 100 different ways to share the gospel and put it in our strategy plan. There was a quote on the wall that touched my heart: "How many people in your city will hear the gospel today?" We prayed and studied the Bible every day to ask God to give us a strategy for how to spread the gospel as quickly as possible and for people to turn to the Lord.

We continued to read the Bible and pray daily until one day, in the middle of the night, we suddenly realized the best strategy for evangelism is in Jesus's Great Commission! We've known this Great Commission (Matthew 28:19-20) since we were children, memorizing this passage of scripture. We were even able to sing it as a song. But in that moment, we discovered that we had never really followed his Great Commission!

## THE GREAT COMMISSION

Jesus said to them: "Therefore go and make disciples of all nations, baptizing them in the name of the Father and of the Son and of the Holy Spirit, and teaching them to obey everything I have commanded you. And surely I am with you always, to the very end of the age" (Matthew 28:19-20).

## THE SIX MAIN POINTS

### 1. Go, not Come

The beginning of Jesus's Great Commission is the command, "Go!" But instead our traditional practice has always been to say, "Come!" We are always inviting people to come to our church, come to our fellowship, or come to our group. To invite people to come may be our common practice, but Jesus said we are to go and find lost persons.

If we do not go, how can we lead people to the Lord? Today, everyone has their road that they must take, so if we do not go, how can we find them? "Go" is a key concept. As long as we "go," we will be able to do things. If we just stay in one place, people will not automatically come to us.

We cannot just wait in the church, nor can we wait for someone to come to our small group at home – they will not come automatically. So the first command is, "Go!" Friends, let us decide to go now! As soon as you go out, you will see the way that the Lord has opened for you. When you go out, you will see those who need you. If you stay, you will miss the opportunity to change or influence them. Staying does not demonstrate an obedient heart towards the authority of Christ.

## 2. Everyone, not just some

Jesus said that all nations - that is every individual, should receive the gospel, become his disciple. But when we used to share the gospel, we would limit those with whom we would share. Even when we were handing out gospel tracts on the streets, we chose the people to whom we handed the tracts. We were wrong; we should offer the gospel to everyone. This requires us to stretch our vision. We must go beyond our limited vision to the Great Commission vision that God has given to us.

Remember Jesus's parable of the sower? The sower was a farmer, and he should have known which parts of the field were ready and good. But this farmer did not follow conventional wisdom. He spread seeds into every corner of the property. He scattered it everywhere.

Yes, some seed fell on rocky ground; some fell on the road; there was seed among the thorns. However, some seed fell on good soil, and its yield increased by 30 times, 60 times, even 100 times! It is our duty to sow the seeds broadly by sharing the gospel everywhere, but the growth of the seed comes from the power of the Holy Spirit.

When Jesus sent the 70 disciples to share the gospel in Luke chapter 10, Jesus gave them a strategy of evangelism: "Whichever house you enter first say, 'Peace to this house.' If someone who promotes peace is there (a person of peace), your peace will rest on them; if not, it will return to you (You are then the person of peace)." A "person of peace" is like the seed that was sown in good soil, reaping a harvest that is a 100 times greater! If we limit the persons we share the gospel with, and don't share with every individual, we will miss these persons of peace.

## 3. A disciple, not just a church member

Jesus wants us to make all people (that is, all mankind) his disciples. Jesus did not say that a person can be merely a believer, Christian, brethren, church member, fellowship member, etc. Jesus said it very clearly – disciple the nations!

If we just make a person a church member, Christian, or fellowship member, we are not meeting the command of Jesus. He commanded us to make everyone his disciple. Disciples are true learners. They follow the Master's footsteps and learn all the Master's skills until they can complete their training and become a Master themselves. This is what it means to be a disciple.

---

### The Tianyun Church

This congregation is an outreach-oriented church located in a group of factories. The church desired to share the gospel with factory workers all over the area. After about a year, only 70 persons were attending their church, they felt progress was slow. So the church invited us to give them T4T training.

After we used the small group training method to train them, we encouraged them to return to each factory to train other factory workers (share the gospel with them and train them into a trainer that trains others).

After three months, we went back to visit them and asked the church leader how the last few weeks had gone. He told us that in just the last month, they have had three to four hundred workers believe in Jesus. It's wonderful! Now they were obeying the Great Commission, training others to become trainers! Because of this the gospel spread very rapidly.

Thank God!

So we should not just bring people to believe in the Lord, become a church member, a Christian, etc., but we must train them to become a trainer (a true disciple) who can train others. We have to train everyone to become a trainer (Training For Trainers). We are convinced that every Christian, even a person who has just decided to believe in Christ, who cannot yet train others, is but a nominal Christian. It is not until one can train others that they can grow into a true disciple.

## 4. Tell your own story   — baptism as testimony

Jesus said to baptize in the name of the Father, the Son and the Holy Spirit. We all know that baptism is a very important testimony as Christians. So, we must train everyone to tell their own story. In many areas, the environment may not allow you to evangelize, but nowhere in the world will you be restricted from sharing your story. So, we need to train everyone to be ready to tell own story in order to share Jesus's love.

## 5. Train others

Jesus said, "Teach them to observe all that I have commanded you." If we are only bringing people to Christ and letting them become fellow church members, our work is not complete. We must train them into disciples who are also able to train others. Only then will we have completed Jesus's Great Commission. So it is not just training, but training them to the point where they take action to train others.

## 6. Obey

This point is so important. Without obedience there are no results. Once we obey our mission from the Great Commission, we can get the greatest blessing from God and a special promise from Matthew 28:20. Jesus said, "And surely I will be with you always, to the very end of the age."

How Jesus taught and trained us is how we should teach and train others. The Lord shared his gospel with us, so we too must share the gospel with others. We must teach others to obey the Lord's word. This is an extremely important truth; for having the Lord's presence is totally different from the absence of the Lord.

So if we want to receive Christ's greatest promise, we must obey the Lord's mandate, and the Lord will be with us until the end of the world!

## SAVED AND LOST

So we put "Training For Trainers" in our master plan. We also wrote that there are only two kinds of people in the world: the lost and the saved. To the lost, we will share the love of Jesus, leading them to believe in Jesus, and immediately train them to become trainers who train others. To the Christians, we determined to train them as trainers to share the gospel and train others to do the same.

We calculated how many people we thought we could lead to Christ each day, each week, and each month over the next three years. We would also immediately train them to lead others to Jesus, and at the same time have them train the new believers. As such we wrote down that if T4T is feasible, we would not need the other 99 evangelism methods.

We then set our end vision: to lead 18,000 people to Christ in three years and begin 200 new churches. Then, we handed in our three-year master plan. This figure was really huge, was it not? Our training director read our master plan and said it looks like a very good plan, but we would have to see what the results would be. We knew he did not believe it was possible, but we were excited to return to our new mission field in November of 2000.

## THE FIRST TRAINING

Our first training took place in a small church in a very rural area with only 57 members, of whom 30 took part in our training. These 30 were very excited. They said they were from a small village and there were no outsiders to train them. They were extremely glad we could come help them. We challenged them to share the gospel in Jesus's Great Commission, but they raised their hands and said, "We know we need to share the gospel, but we do not know how to share."

I replied, "Yes, I understand. There are actually only two reasons why Christians don't share the gospel today: first, there are so many people, they don't know who to share with or where to start. Second, they don't know what to share." I looked at the 30 trainees and said, "Today, I am here to help you resolve these issues."

So I gave each person a piece of paper and asked them to pray. I told them, "Think of all the people around you, including your family, relatives, neighbors, colleagues, and friends. Anyone you know who is not a Christian, write down their names and make that your name list." I gave them about 15 minutes and almost everyone had written 20 to 30 names. I recall one man wrote more than 70 names!

Then, I told them, "You have a responsibility from today onwards – you have to pray for them. Not just mention their names to the Father, but to pray for them specifically and in detail. If the first name on your name list is your uncle (for example, Uncle John), tell the Father where Uncle John is now, what his situation is, why you're concerned about him. Then, ask the Holy Spirit to prepare Uncle John's heart, move his heart, give him a soft heart, and a hungry heart. At the same time, pray for yourselves, that the Holy Spirit will prepare your heart and give you the wisdom, the opportunity, and words to share the gospel with your uncle. Start with prayer and the Holy Spirit will begin his work and will be with you."

Then I asked them to circle the names of five persons they want to immediately share the gospel with. This group would be their first group. Then they were to circle the second group of five people, then another five in the third group. I told them, "Starting tomorrow, you have to share the gospel with at least five persons every week. Now we have answered your first question: you have a list and also a target group. You know who to share with and thus the first question has been resolved."

"Your second question is that you do not know what to share. The answer is very simple: share your own story." So, I gave each of them another piece of paper, asking them to write down their own story. I told them, "Your story can not be too long, because everyone is very busy nowadays and won't have time to listen to a long story. Your story should be about a page; about a minute and a half is enough."

"Your story should be divided into three parts: the first part being how you lived before you knew the Lord. An example would be if I used to be a person without joy and peace or if I had a short temper. Write down your situation. The second part would be under what circumstances did you come to believe in Jesus? The third part would be now that you have accepted Jesus, what joy or peace do you have in your life?" I gave them 15 minutes to write down their story.

Afterwards we asked them to stand up and read their story out loud five times, speaking loudly to block out others. Anyone can write down their own story, but not everyone can tell their story fluently to others. So I led them to practice and memorize their story.

I told them to form groups of two so that they can practice with each other and have each other listen to their story. I told them, "When you listen to one another's story it's your responsibility to help one another. First, listen to see if that person's story makes sense. If you cannot understand it, then others will not understand it. Second, if there are too many biblical or religious terms, take them out because non-Christians will most likely not understand. Third, make sure their story is interesting as it is only useful if people are willing to listen."

Then I said, "Now you have the list – you know who you can share with. You also have a personal story – you can share your testimony. But I tell you, though your story may be touching or moving, simply listening to your story is not enough. They do not yet know Jesus and do not understand the Truth. So when you finish your story, you must go on to tell the story of Jesus. Here are seven simple lessons. Tonight, I want to teach you the first lesson: the assurance of salvation!"

We handed them each a copy of the first lesson and told them, "Now I will teach you slowly. Write down every Bible verse I give you, every example, and every sentence. After I have finished teaching, you must immediately practice teaching each other, because starting tomorrow you will have to teach others." So I slowly taught them and afterwards had them practice with each other until they were comfortable and had the confidence to teach others the next day.

We then gave each person five copies of the first lesson and said to them, "Starting tomorrow morning, find the first group of five people on your list and tell them your story and the story of Jesus. You do not need to bring them together. It can be done at home, on the street, under a tree, or in a restaurant. Tell anyone you meet your story and the story of Jesus. If you cannot find the first group of people on your list, you need to go to the second or third group to share the gospel. You must share with at least five people every week!"

Then I prayed for them. After the prayer, I told them "There is one thing that is very important: you do not need their permission when you share the gospel. You do not need to ask them if they want to listen. We use to ask in a very polite manner: 'Do you want to listen to Jesus's story? Would you let me share the gospel with you?' If they answer, 'I do not want to hear,' then you have lost the chance to share the gospel with them and the gospel door would be closed." I shared with them my own experience.

## EVANGELISM WITHOUT PERMISSION

For more than 20 years, I was the director of pastoral care at a government hospital in Hong Kong. Every day when I visited the patients, I would always greet them and ask, "How are you today? Are you feeling better?" Then, I would introduce myself, "I am the chaplain at this hospital. May I share with you the love of Jesus?" Up to that point, every individual would politely respond to my questions. However, once they would hear the conversation shifting to Jesus, many would immediately say, "I do not want to hear" or "I am very tired, don't bother me."

This was a government hospital and I was a volunteer chaplain. So if I wanted to continue to evangelize, they might ring the bell and say, "This person is bothering me!" It would affect my chances to continue evangelism in the hospital. At that time, my records showed that only one or two people in every 15 beds would listen to my testimony. The rest would not listen. I did not have the opportunity to share the gospel and it made my heart very sad.

It wasn't until one day, when my wife and I were in Taiwan that I changed my approach. At breakfast, the people of Taiwan like to drink soy milk. Each time my wife and I ordered two bowls of hot soy milk, they would ask whether or not we wanted to add an egg to the milk. It was very delicious, but it was too expensive for me. As such, every time I would say no to the egg.

But one time, when we went to eat breakfast, I ordered my usual two bowls of soy milk. Suddenly, the owner asked me, "One egg or two eggs?" Without thinking, I replied, "One egg!"

When I sat down, Grace asked me, "Why did you add an egg today?" I responded, "Oh this owner did not ask me whether or not I wanted to add an egg, he directly asked me one egg or two eggs?" I started to pay close attention to him and every customer who ordered soy milk, he would always ask, "One egg or two eggs?" Every customer would naturally respond with one egg or two eggs. Nobody said no. I told Grace, "This man is very smart. He never asked anyone if they wanted to add an egg but simply offered "one egg or two eggs?"

We then talked about how we should give the good news directly to people and not ask them if they wanted it or not. We thought of a story Jesus told in the Bible. The Good Shepherd had 100 sheep and lost one. He left behind the 99 to find the lost sheep. What did he say to the sheep when he found him? Did he say,

## A Fruitful Old Woman

An old woman from a large city came to faith in Jesus. She got involved in a traditional church, but they did not teach her how to share the gospel with others.

One day she returned to her small hometown and learned that they had a T4T training group there. When she joined the training, the team trainer told her she should start to witness, evangelize, and start her own training group. So, she started to use the T4T process with others to share the gospel and start her own T4T training group.

After a year her Big Trainers sent her to another town to do more T4T training. Within a year at that town, she launched over 78 training groups. At the same time, she sent the trainers within those training groups to other cities to start their own training groups. In this way, the gospel spread far and wide.

Thanks be to God!

"Little sheep, would you like to come home with me? Would it be okay if I introduce you to our home?"

Certainly not! This sheep was his. It was lost, but now it is found! He should immediately take the sheep home and celebrate the occasion, right? Because the sheep belonged to him, it should go home with him.

Today, everyone in the world is created by our Heavenly Father and belongs to him, but they are just lost. When we face these lost people today, how can we stand outside the door and ask, "Do you want to hear about the good news of going back home to the Heavenly Father? May I introduce Jesus to you?" We were wrong! We should give the good news directly to them and lead them back to our Father's house.

When I returned to Hong Kong and visited the patients in the hospital, I changed my approach. I still asked them, "How are you today?" But then, I would continue with, "You do not know me, but I used to be a person with anger issues and quarrel with people every day. I would often get angry and quarrel with my wife." Everyone loves to listen to another person's bad story. No one would say, "I do not want to hear this." I would then share how Jesus came into my life and changed me; how my wife and I now enjoy a very beautiful life filled with joy and peace.

After hearing my story most of those I shared with exclaimed, "Wow, that is amazing! That is simply a miracle!" I would not wait, but immediately give them the first lesson: the assurance of God's salvation.

The first sentence is: Praise the Heavenly Father, you are also a child of our Heavenly Father. You can also have the same life filled with joy and peace! After I finish sharing my story, I would immediately share the story of Jesus. With this minor change: not asking them whether or not they wanted to hear the gospel, but directly sharing the gospel with them, my record increased to more than 10 out of every 15 patients would listen to my complete testimony and Jesus's story. As a result more people believed in Jesus. So in evangelism, never ask for permission when sharing the gospel. Just share with them directly.

So I encouraged the 30 farmers, "Starting from tomorrow morning, share your story with whomever you meet and then follow it with the story of Jesus. The Holy Spirit will be with you. I will teach you the second lesson when you come back next week." All 30 came back the next week and I asked "Who shared the gospel last week?" Only 11 raised their hands.

We asked them to share their gospel results. Some people said that they tried to share the gospel with about three people, but no one accepted Jesus. One said he successfully led only one man to believe in Jesus. Then, an old farmer raised his hand and said, "Pastor, last week I led 11 men to believe in the Lord!"

Amazing! I invited him to stand up and give his testimony. He stood up and said, "I have believed in the Lord for more than two decades, but no one has ever taught me how to really share the good news of Christ. Last week I learned how to tell my story and the story of Jesus. There are 34 families in my village, and I knocked on all 34 doors in one week. I shared with each of them my story and the story of Jesus. A total of 11 believed in Jesus."

Praise the Father, this farmer is a "person of peace." To be honest, if I were to choose a leader, I would have never chosen this old farmer because I could barely understand him. However, God chose him.

## FROM GENERATION TO GENERATION

That day, I taught them the second lesson (understanding prayer). After they were taught, I told them to practice with each other until they were skilled and confident enough to teach others.

After that, I gave them a new assignment, "Last week, if you brought three people to believe in Jesus, then I'll give you three copies of Lesson 2. This is because after you go home, you will be teaching Lesson 2 to these new believers.

At the same time, I will also be giving you 15 copies of the first lesson. This is because when you go back to teach your new believers the second lesson, you will need them to write down their name lists and stories. Then you will give each of them five copies of Lesson 1. Have them practice with each other, so that they may be able to train other people. How I teach you is how you should teach them so that it can continue from generation to generation.

I do not want you to bring other people to my small group. It is not my desire to grow my small group larger because right now I am training you to become a trainer, a disciple. So I want you to train them, because if you start bringing others to our small group, you will not go to train others."

So every week I trained them in Lesson 1 and then gave them enough material so that they could train others. I would also make sure to provide them with enough materials to train the next generation of believers.

We started this training at the end of November 2000. By February 2001, after only three months, these 30 farmers had led more than 200 individuals to believe in Jesus and started 27 small groups.

Thank the Lord! During our three years in Hong Kong, we had led less than 200 persons to faith in Jesus Christ. But now that we followed Jesus's Great Commission pattern and trained them as trainers (disciples), in three months, we had already seen results that surpassed our three years in Hong Kong!

Over the next few months we led T4T training in every city, town, and district, training every disciple to become a trainer. We found that the Heavenly Father was at work in all places. In every place, there was always a person of peace prepared for us. God can and does use many different kinds of people as persons of peace – farmers, doctors, priests, factory workers, university professors, even illiterate people and officers!

By the end of 2001, after only 13 months, the 30 farmers from the first group had already shared the gospel in 17 different cities leading more than 10,000 people to believe in Jesus and had established 906 small discipleship groups. These kinds of results were not something we could have imagined. The old farmer became the pastor of a small church. He told us that he got up at 5:00 a.m. every morning, prayed for two hours, and then went to work in the fields until 5:00 p.m. in the afternoon when he took a bath and had supper. Then every night he would ride his motorcycle to go train three to four small groups.

He encouraged everyone in his church to start their own training group. After two years, this small church bought the two pieces of land on both sides of the original church building and built a large gathering place to accommodate 500 members. The old farmer said to me, "I changed the service time of our church from the morning to 1:00 p.m." When I asked him why, he said, "Many of the elderly and children live too far away. They are unable to walk to the church. So every Sunday morning I send more than 40 brothers to a different village on motorcycles to lead Sunday worship. Every Sunday we use a large tank or the river to baptize many people."

"Thank the Lord," he said, "for he increases the number of saved people every day! On Sunday afternoons around 1:00 p.m., we welcome all the brothers and sisters back to the home church to praise and worship God together. I then encourage them to share a testimonial of what God is doing at the different locations. I then spend about 15 minutes on vision casting to encourage them." You see God's strategy is better than mine. God is the best at choosing workers for his Kingdom. Let us come together and praise God!

When many people start to use T4T, they do not understand the difference between training a new believer and training a long-time Christian. The chart below illustrates the subtle differences.

| | NEW BELIEVER | LONG-TIME CHRISTIAN |
|---|---|---|
| WEEK 1 | Your own testimony + Jesus Story (1st Lesson)<br><br>After they make the decision to follow Jesus, immediately teach them how to share their testimony of how they were saved. This includes:<br><br>1. What they have heard.<br><br>2. Why it moved them.<br><br>3. What feelings do they have in their heart?<br><br>4. Their expectations for their new life.<br><br>Then, pray for them and tell them to share their story with at least five persons by the next week. Finally, set a meeting time for the next week. | Share the Great Commission - vision cast.<br><br>Have them write their name list and story. Then, teach them the first lesson (Jesus Story - Assurance of Salvation). Have them practice how to teach others the first lesson. Set goals for next week. |
| WEEK 2 | Share the Great Commission - vision cast. Teach them the second lesson. Have them write out their name list and story. Have them practice how to teach others the first lesson. Set goals for next week. | Use the three-thirds process (see Chapter 8) to teach the second lesson. During vision casting time, share the Heavenly Father's heart. Have them practice, review their name list, and set goals. |
| WEEK 3 | Same training as long-time Christians.<br><br>Use the three-thirds process (see Chapter 8). | Same training as for new believers.<br><br>Use the three-thirds process. |

## Discussion Questions

- What are the main points in Jesus's Great Commission?

1. Go not come  2. Everyone  3. disciple not member
4. Testimony  5. Train others  6. obey

- How do I obey and practice the Great Commission of Jesus?

Share my story + Jesus' story. Train the ones who accept Jesus to do the same.

- How do I solve the problem of Christians who do not share the gospel? Train them.

- What are the two kinds of persons in the world?

Saved + lost

- How do we share the gospel?

Just do it - pray for the people who are in your circle of influence. Then share.

- What is a trainer?

a disciple who trains others

- What is the difference between disciples and believers?

people who train others

know Jesus but don't necessarily train others

# 2

# The Heavenly Father's Heart

Church Planting Movements (CPMs) are the rapid multiplication of new churches that sweep through a people group or population. When we understand the ways and means of Church Planting Movements, we should begin training Christians immediately and make everyone we contact become a "trainer."

We do not do typical training nor do we just do leadership training. Rather, we train people to become "trainers of trainers" As Paul taught Timothy, "...the things you have heard me say in the presence of many witnesses entrust to reliable people who will also be qualified to teach others" (2 Timothy 2:2).

We must understand that the Heavenly Father's heart is that all men be saved, starting with one's own family. The Father loves you, and has saved you and through you wants to save your family! When you really understand the heart of the Father, you will have the confidence, the ability, and the assurance you need to share the gospel with your family and friends. You should never give up until they are saved!

## NOAH AND HIS FAMILY

God instructed Noah to build the ark (Genesis 6-7). He told him to warn the world, for only those who entered the ark would be saved. Noah preached for 120 years, but no one believed him except, his wife, sons, and daughters-in-law who listened to his words and were saved.

## LOT AND HIS FAMILY

When Sodom and Gomorrah sinned before God, God determined to destroy the two cities. But through the relationship between God and Abraham, God cared for Lot and his family (Genesis 19:12-23). Unfortunately, Lot's sons-in-law did not believe him (perhaps Lot's witness at home was poor.) So our witness at home is very important or else in critical moments, we will not be able to save our family. In the end, only Lot and his two daughters were saved. But this was not God's desire. God's heart was to save Lot and use him to save all of his family.

## RAHAB AND HER FAMILY

Rahab saved the two Israeli spies and asked them to protect the lives of her and her family from the attack on her city. The Father saved Rahab's family through her (Joshua 2:17-20).

## THE DEMONIAC AND HIS VILLAGE

When Jesus drove the demons out of this man, he sat at the feet of Jesus listening to his sermon. But the people in the village were afraid and asked Jesus to leave. This former demoniac wanted to follow Jesus, but Jesus told him to return to his hometown (Mark 5:12-20). To do what? To tell his story.

Jesus said, "Go home to your own people and tell them how much the Lord has done for you, and how he has had mercy on you." The man went back to his homeland called the Decapolis, made up of 10 towns, to testify to his people.

We see in the Bible, many people opposed Jesus, but later when Jesus went to the Decapolis, people came out from the villages to welcome him and said, "We have been waiting for you for a long time." Thanks to the Heavenly Father for he loved the Gerasene demoniac and saved him, and through his witness saved many throughout the Decapolis.

## A T4T-Trained Factory Worker

During one of our trainings, a worker heard the good news that our Heavenly Father wanted to save him, and through him save all the people related to him.

He was an orphan with no family or friends, so he thought, who would be considered the people related to me? He thought of his colleagues that lived in the same dorm and the Heavenly Father began to prepare his heart.

He began to pray for them and witnessed to them. After listening to him, they all laughed and ignored him. However, he continued to pray for them every day in hopes that one day, they would listen to his testimony.

On Christmas Eve night, he was preparing to go to attend a special church service. Suddenly, one of his roommates asked him, "Are you going to church? Can I go with you?"

The factory worker was delighted. He finally had a person willing to go to church with him. They both listened to the message and received it with joy. When the pastor called out for people to make a decision, his friend raised his hand to accept Jesus and went to the front. The worker was very happy he was able to lead people to the Lord.

When they return to the dormitory, they found that their colleagues were not inside the dormitory. After about 10 minutes, they heard the sound of laughter outside and saw all the other men coming back together.

Upon entering the room, their colleagues asked these two friends, "Do you know where we went tonight?" The two friends responded, "Did you guys go celebrate Christmas with a big dinner?"

They responded, "No, actually we all went to your church. And when the pastor called for a decision – we all went to the front, but the church was so full, we couldn't find you.

Tonight we were all saved by the blood of Jesus. Would you please tell us more about Jesus who came to earth to save us?"

Thanks be to God, for God saved this factory worker and through him, saved a whole dorm full of people.

## CORNELIUS AND HIS HOUSEHOLD

Cornelius invited Peter to his house, and invited all his close friends. When Peter began to speak, the Holy Spirit fell upon them, and all of them were saved (Acts 10:23-25).

## LYDIA AND HER FAMILY

After becoming a believer, Lydia immediately led her entire family to be saved, and invited Paul and Silas to stay in her home (Acts 16:14-15).

## PHILIPPIAN JAILER AND HIS HOUSEHOLD

When the officer was saved, he immediately brought Paul and Silas to his home even though it was the middle of the night. That very night, he and all the people that belonged to him were saved (Acts 16:31). Thank the Lord, for the Church in Philippi started with this family.

**The Heavenly Father also loves you and wants to save your whole family through you.**

*Discussion Questions*

- What is the Heavenly Father's heart?
  *that all men might be saved*

- What biblical examples reveal that the Heavenly Father's call, election, salvation, and blessing are for the whole family?
  *Noah, Abraham + Lot, Rahab, Lydia, Cornelius*
- Can you find more evidence in the Bible?
  *Joseph*

- Do you care about every member of your family?
  *yes*

- Parents, how do you treat your child after you give birth?
  *care for them, keep them safe, provide for them*

# The Kingdom Worker

T4T is very simple. The main point is to comply with the Great Commission of Jesus and to practice Jesus's strategy. But the most important aspect of this strategy is to get other workers (trainers) involved in the Great Commission. Therefore, T4T is focused on the workers training and development into a disciple.

The workers of the Kingdom are pleasing to the Lord. They obey the task and understand the Father's heart. Because of this, they have the Holy Spirit working through them.

Jesus said in Matthew 9:37-38 "The harvest is plentiful, but the workers are few. Ask the Lord of the harvest, therefore, to send out workers into his harvest field."

"Send out workers?" – yes, we need workers for the harvest, but the question is what kind of workers? In the 10th chapter of Matthew, Jesus sent the twelve Apostles to share the gospel with his blessings, strategy, and power. In chapter 13, Jesus shared seven Kingdom parables, through which he revealed the work of the Heavenly Kingdom, their attitudes, responsibilities, and qualifications. This is the strategy Jesus gave to his Kingdom workers.

The Bible tells us that God created heaven and earth in six ays. In that time, he also created the first people, Adam and Eve, to work with God in managing the world. But unfortunately, they failed after a short time and gave the power of management to Satan. So Satan became the king of the world.

So God changed his plan. His original plan was to have men and women work with God, manage the world, praise and enjoy God's abundant preparation. But mankind failed. Even though they failed, God still loved mankind with his unparalleled love.

So God planned for his one and only beloved Son to come into the world and die for our sins, to redeem us from our sins and to rebuild the Kingdom of God in this world and to take men back from the power of Satan. So when the Son of God came into the world, his mission was to rebuild the Kingdom of Heaven on Earth, so that all mankind could leave Satan's kingdom and enter the Kingdom of God.

## THE KINGDOM OF HEAVEN IS NEAR

The first time Jesus went out to preach the gospel, it is recorded in Mark 1:15: "The time has come," he said. "The Kingdom of God has come near. Repent and believe the good news!"

When Jesus taught his disciples how to pray, he said, "...Thy Kingdom come..." So Jesus's mission is to rebuild the Kingdom of Heaven on earth, and to enter into the Kingdom of God to live a new life.

In Matthew chapter 13, Jesus used seven parables to describe the Kingdom. He spoke of the range of the Kingdom of Heaven and the attitude, faith, duty, and commitment of the workers in the Kingdom. Many people read these parables of the Kingdom of Heaven and think all that Jesus is doing is giving different angles to describe the Kingdom of Heaven. But Jesus is doing more. Jesus is also giving us the best strategy to expand the Kingdom of Heaven and cultivate the tactics of building the Heavenly Kingdom's workers.

Jesus spoke of the Kingdom of Heaven in his own way and order. In the first four parables, Jesus spoke to everyone. It was only after Jesus and his disciples entered the house together that he told his disciples the latter three parables. So Jesus offered different meanings and teachings to different audiences. When we look at the parable of the Heavenly Kingdom, we should view them through Jesus's eyes; only then can we understand the mind of Jesus.

First, we have to take a self-evaluation of our own life and ask, "What is the Kingdom of Heaven to me? What does the Heavenly Kingdom have to do with me? Am I someone at work in the Kingdom of Heaven? Or am I just someone standing outside the Kingdom every day, discussing with people how beautiful and great the Kingdom is without ever having worked in the Kingdom?"

If we only have empty knowledge that is not brought to life through the experience of working in the Kingdom of Heaven, then we are simply standing outside holding empty knowledge of the Kingdom. Jesus said, "Not everyone who says to me, 'Lord,

## Five Lost Cows

A farmer lost five cows. Though his family looked for a long time, they were unable to find them. After a few days, they felt despair. The farmer told the story to his T4T team trainer, and asked this brother in Christ what he should do. His trainer told him, you should go home, shut the door, and kneel down to pray in a quiet room for God to help you.

So, he went home, entered his room, closed the door, knelt down and prayed. After praying for a time, as he was standing up, he heard someone knocking at the door. They asked him, "Outside of the village is a big ravine. There are some cows there. Maybe you should take a look and see if they are your cows." He immediately ran to have a look. Sure enough all five of his cows were there, not one was missing.

He was very grateful to God and began to share his story: "I relied on my own resources and could not find these cows. But after hearing the recommendations of my T4T trainer, I went home, shut the door, knelt down and prayed. God heard my prayer, and immediately I found my lost cows."

In a spirit of thanksgiving, he presented the price of a cow to the church and asked that the money be dedicated to the T4T training centers. In the next one year, he led more than 100 people to Christ.

Praise God!

Lord,' will enter the Kingdom of Heaven, but only the one who does the will of my Father who is in heaven" (Matthew 7:21).

Therefore, we should first ask ourselves, where am I? I may say that I am a Christian, but if it is only knowledge of the truth and I have never really worked in the Kingdom of God, then I am just a nominal Christian and not a true Kingdom citizen.

Many Christians today talk about how beautiful and desirable the Kingdom of Heaven is, but it is such a pity that they have never been a worker within the Kingdom!

Jesus warned, "Woe to you, teachers of the law and Pharisees, you hypocrites! You shut the door of the Kingdom of Heaven in people's faces. You yourselves do not enter, nor will you let those enter who are trying to" (Matthew 23:13). Jesus also said, "Therefore I tell you that the Kingdom of God will be taken away from you and given to a people who will produce its fruit" (Matthew 21:43). Therefore, T4T trains everyone to become a worker in the Kingdom.

Let's look together at Jesus's Kingdom-building strategy.

## 1. THE PARABLE OF THE SOWER

The Kingdom of Heaven is like a farmer going out to sow his field. The farmer should know when and where the field is ready, but instead the farmer goes and spreads the seeds everywhere. Why? Because the message of the Kingdom of Heaven is for everyone.

Some may be in dry land, some in the roadside, some in the thicket of thorns – the results are not always good. However, some seed ends up on good soil and is very fruitful. This parable of Jesus states that it is our duty to sow the seeds broadly and we should not limit where and when we sow.

We should sow the seeds of his Kingdom to the whole world. We must extend the Kingdom of God as much as we can without limitations. The gospel of the Kingdom should be shared with everyone. The seed may not be fruitful for the time being, but once the Holy Spirit begins to work, the seed will reproduce a hundred fold. Jesus taught that the gospel of this Kingdom is for everyone because God wants everyone to be saved and for none to perish.

## 2. WHEAT AND WEEDS

The Kingdom of Heaven has many workers who work hard and grow a lot of wheat, but in the middle of the night the enemy planted weeds among the wheat. Seeing this, the workers asked the Master if they should pull out the weeds.

The Master said, "'No,' he answered, 'because while you are pulling the weeds, you may uproot the wheat with them. Let both grow together until the harvest. At that time I will tell the harvesters: First collect the weeds and tie them in bundles to be burned; then gather the wheat and bring it into my barn.'" This parable tells us that even when we work hard, and are not on guard or fall asleep, the enemy is going to come and destroy some of our work.

In fact, no matter how watchful we are, the enemy will come. The enemy will never give up undermining our work. But our duty is to concentrate on our work, to take care of our field and not to suspend our ministry because of the enemy's disruption.

But today many people want to criticize the work of others, always finding this thing wrong or that thing wrong in their church, or institution, or small group. They think: This person isn't right, that person is unfaithful. However, I am a faithful and righteous man, so I must clean up my church, institution, or small group, and correct the other person's fault.

I tell you, the Lord Jesus wants us to concentrate on doing our own work. Do not waste time looking at the faults of others. Do not spend time criticizing and correcting others. Because when we remove the weeds, we are likely to injure the wheat. Likewise, when you want to clean up your church, institution, or small group, you may also hurt other brothers and sisters! Therefore, the attitude of the Kingdom worker is this: concentrate on your own work; trust the power to the Lord, because in the end of days, God will personally judge. Those that do evil will be destroyed by fire; and the righteous will shine like the sun in their Father's Kingdom (Matthew 13: 41-43)!

## 3. MUSTARD SEED

The Kingdom of Heaven is like a mustard seed planted in the ground, it can grow into a big tree. The mustard seed is one of the smallest seeds, but it can grow into a big tree. This should remind us that we should not underestimate the small initial work, because through the blessing of the Lord, there will be a great effect.

Here the Lord reminds us that there are birds that may come and stay in the tree. This we need to be careful of, because the birds will eat the fruit of the tree. Therefore, when our work is fruitful, we must protect it. I often see fruit farmers wrap up each fruit with a bag in order to protect these hard-won fruit so it does not get eaten by birds or taken away by monkeys. Likewise, we must protect our fruit and protect every fruit of the Spirit.

The best way to protect the fruit is to train and equip the new believers. Being born again is not enough; we should train them immediately to become a trainer (disciple). It's just like when we give birth to a child, we will not just give birth to them. We will nurture and care for them until they are grown up and are able to stand on their own. We all hope that our children can succeed, and end up in a better situation than us. Only with a good education and seeing a good example can they live healthy lives with vitality, marry in the future, and naturally bring the next healthy generation.

## Salvation at a Funeral

Once an 85-year-old sister passed away and more than 50 people came to believe in Jesus at her funeral. How did this happen?

During her lifetime, this dear old saint loved Jesus and often witnessed to the people, preaching the love of Jesus. She also helped many people in the vicinity, including her relatives and friends. She always testified to them, telling them of Jesus' love. She used all her strength and resources to help them.

When they came to her funeral, the people came close and saw her face, it seemed luminous and looked so serene. During the funeral, they suddenly saw a light come down from heaven and shine on her casket. She looked like an angel. They again remembered her sharing her testimony and her lifetime love of Jesus, so 50 people decided to believe in Jesus that day.

Praise God!

We are to treat the new fruit of the harvest with the same care and teaching, not simply pass them on to others (such as pastors or deacons). We must nurture and train them ourselves, because they are our spiritual children. We have this God-given responsibility. This is the only way they can be protected and not be captured by Satan.

## 4. LEAVEN

The Kingdom of Heaven is like yeast (leaven) that is added to the dough. It will eventually affect the whole lump of dough. Here again we see a metaphor about the Kingdom of Heaven that can bear "fruit." But we should note that whenever the leaven is mentioned in the Bible, it is not good. In the Old Testament, Moses taught us that in our sacrifices, we are not to use yeast, but to use salt. Jesus also reminded us to guard against the leaven of the Pharisees.

Looking back over the past 2000 years, the Kingdom can seem to have been growing fast, but we can also see many false teachings, heresies, and divisions. Therefore when we work in the Kingdom of Heaven, it is important to have careful cultivation of the believers. We need to be sure to enable them to become disciples (trainers) of the Lord. The main teachings we should share is that (1) the Bible is the Word of God, and (2) to "correctly handle the Word of truth" (2 Timothy 2:15). This is the only way to guard the Kingdom of God and the Kingdom of God's people.

The above four parables are what Jesus said to all the people and to everyone. After this, Jesus sent the multitudes away, went into the house with his disciples, and shared only with them the following three parables.

## 5. THE HIDDEN TREASURE

The Kingdom of Heaven is like a hidden treasure. When one finds it, they would sell all they have in order to obtain the treasure (Matthew 13:44).

## 6. THE PEARL OF GREAT PRICE

The Kingdom of Heaven is like a precious pearl, and when a man finds it, he sells all that he has, to buy this precious pearl (Matthew 13:46).

We should look at these two parables together. Many people think that the Kingdom of Heaven can be found; that it is something that we should give up everything for then sell all that we have so that we can buy this treasure or buy this pearl and enter the Kingdom of Heaven. However, we should look at these parables from Jesus' standpoint. How can we enter the Kingdom of Heaven today? Would we be able to afford to buy the entrance to the Kingdom? No, this is a misunderstanding! Entering the Kingdom of Heaven is by the grace of the Father; it is free! It is not something we can sell everything to buy because we can never afford the price to enter the Kingdom of Heaven. Today, we freely enter heaven because of the grace of the Father.

Jesus is the one who paid the price for us – his life. It cost our Lord Jesus dearly. He forsook everything, descended from heaven, and paid for all our sins with his own life so that we may enter into the Kingdom of the Son, and have a new life! What is the treasure and pearl? Who is the treasure and pearl? Who is looking for it?

Our Lord Jesus is the one searching for his treasure and pearl. All of us have already received the rich and unconditional blessing – becoming the children of God. Should we not also become the treasure and pearl in the hand of Jesus? But how can we become this precious treasure, this pearl? The answer is in the next parable.

## 7. A NET CAST INTO THE SEA

In this parable the Kingdom of Heaven is compared to a net that is cast into the sea (Matthew 13:47). When the net is pulled back, the good is gathered into containers, and the bad is thrown away. This analogy tells us: many people are called but few are chosen.

But how can we become a chosen treasure or pearl? The answer is found in Paul's second letter to Timothy. "In a large house there are articles not only of gold and silver, but also of wood and clay; some are for special purposes and some for common use. Those who cleanse themselves from the latter will be instruments for special purposes, made holy, useful to the Master and prepared to do any good work" (2 Timothy 2:20-21).

There are certainly many different utensils available in your home. You may have many made of wood or clay that are easy to use. However, you would rarely have utensils made of gold and silver or maybe none at all, because wood and clay are cheaper to use and more useful. We may also look at ourselves this way.

We may be very smart, very capable, very experienced, and we can do this and that. But in the Father's eyes, he does not look at how wise and capable you are. In the eyes of God, He looks at whether you are a valuable vessel and whether you are a man after God's will – because God values quality more than quantity.

God sees our heart to serve and not how talented we are. We may feel very useful and very smart, but God cannot use us. So how can we become a valuable vessel that can be used by God? The answer is through "cleansing ourselves" as Paul taught Timothy. This is the last book Paul wrote in his lifetime. He reminds us that we should strive to cleanse ourselves from dishonor so that we can become precious instruments to be used by God.

How do we go about cleansing ourselves? The only way to do this is found in Paul's letter to the Romans. "Therefore, I urge you, brothers and sisters, in view of God's mercy, to offer your bodies as a living sacrifice, holy and pleasing to God—this is your true and proper worship" (Romans 12:1).

We need to let God break us completely; then unreservedly offer ourselves entirely to him, not in part or on a piecemeal basis. Only the sacrificial fire of the Holy Spirit will burn off all dross in our lives in order for us to be truly purified, then we can become vessels of God - God's precious treasures, pearls.

When we truly enter the Kingdom of Heaven, and become good and faithful Kingdom workers, then we are in the hands of the Lord Jesus, his treasured possession!

## BRINGING HEAVEN ON EARTH

1. Once we have been saved, we have already entered the Kingdom of God. Do not just understand the Truth without living it out.

2. To expand the Kingdom of God share the gospel with everyone.

3. Concentrate on serving God, not criticizing others.

4. To protect the fruit we harvest, train them to become trainers.

5. Teach them the Word of righteousness, the holy word of God.

6. Cleanse yourself, be humble, and offer yourself to become the Lord's valuable vessel, treasure and pearl.

7. Praise the Lord! Train every trainer into a loyal, good and insightful servant – a heavenly worker!

## Discussion Questions

• Where do the workers work?

• What is a worker's job? Do you work in the Kingdom of Heaven today?

• What is the attitude of Kingdom workers?

• How do you protect your fruit?

• What is your training material?

• Who is the Father's treasure and pearl?

• How does one become the Father's treasure and pearl?

# 4

# *The Power of the Holy Spirit*

The three most important factors for the success of T4T are: 1) Obey and follow Jesus's Great Commission, 2) understand the Heavenly Father's heart, and 3) work through the power of the Holy Spirit.

You may have all the materials and a good understanding of all the steps and methods of T4T, but if the power of the Holy Spirit is not working through you, then you can do nothing. But what is the power of the Holy Spirit?

One day, a man went to visit his friend. Before he knew it, it was midnight and he had to go home. Because it was already very late, he took a shortcut, which went through a cemetery. Since he had walked through it many times before, he felt he knew the road and thus was not afraid or worried.

That night there was no moonlight and it was very dark. While walking through the cemetery, the man did not see that there was a newly dug grave to be used for a funeral the next day. He accidentally fell into the hole. After falling in, he tried to jump out, but the hole was just too deep. He tried several times to climb out but was unsuccessful. Finally, he gave up and thought to himself that someone would come to help him out the next morning.

A few minutes later another man came along and he also fell into the hole. That person also tried to jump out. After having tried two or three times, he suddenly heard a voice from behind him say, "Don't bother trying to jump out, you won't get out!" Upon hearing that voice, the second man immediately found the strength to leap out of the hole!

This second man's supernatural power is like the power of the Holy Spirit! The man never knew that he had so much potential. As

## A 17-Year-Old Son

One night, before I started a T4T training, there was a 26-year-old young man who had already become the manager of a factory in that area. He came to me and said, "Pastor, my feet really hurt. Would you please pray for me? I know you are a chaplain at the Hong Kong Hospital." I said yes and prayed with him. After the prayer, we started the training.

At the end of the training, he came and said, "Thank you! Because of your prayers, my feet feel much better. Tomorrow morning, I want to invite you to my house."

The next morning, when I went to his house, I found he had a large extended family gathered. In one of their large living rooms, there were around 20 people sitting there. Most of them were smoking and it was a foul environment.

He introduced me saying, "This is my dad's oldest brother, my uncle. He is the chairman of the local Buddhist temple. This is my second uncle and my father is the youngest of three brothers." He then pointed to a young man lying on a table, whose whole body was bowed up and could not be straightened.

He told me, "This is my uncle's only son. He is 17 years old this year. One year ago, my cousin caught a strange disease and became unable to stand up. My uncle has taken him to all the hospitals in this province, and also visited all the different temples to pray and beg for healing but to no avail. Pastor, last night you prayed for my feet and my feet are better. So I told them you are from Hong Kong and serve at the hospital as a chaplain. I hope you can pray for him."

long as the Holy Spirit is with you, you can do things that you thought were impossible –things that you believed you could not do.

In John 14:12 Jesus said, "Very truly I tell you, whoever believes in me will do the works I have been doing, and they will do even greater things than these, because I am going to the Father."

When we first look at this verse, we really do not understand; how can we be compared to Jesus? Jesus is the Son of God and can do miracles. He once fed 5,000 people, another time 4,000 ate food that Jesus provided. He even raised the dead!

Who are we? How could we be compared to Jesus? But our Lord must have had his meaning when he said this. The Lord's meaning is in the last sentence of this verse: "...because I am

---

I said, "I am willing to pray for this young man. However, you must first know Jesus and his power, and accept him as savior, or my prayers are in vain."

After this, I began to share the love of Jesus. After sharing for about 20 minutes, they said, "Okay, okay, we all believe. Would you please pray for him as soon as possible?"

So I knelt down and began to pray for him. When I got up after praying, nothing happened. The young man also did not have any change of feeling. I told them that I would continue to pray for him and that they needed to have faith and learn how to pray for him. I then told them I would come back the following week.

The next week, I went to the T4T training center to do training. Upon arrival, I found it was filled with people. Everyone stood and clapped and I had no idea what had happened.

It was at this time, the uncle came up to me and said, "Pastor, the day after you left, my son stood up. He is now fully recovered! In our whole village, we have 32 families, totaling 69 adults. We are all here and would love it if you could share the good news of Jesus. We would like to hear it and share it with others."

That day, they all decided to believe in Jesus. Praise God! I told them that healing the body is temporary, but the soul is eternal for salvation through Christ.

That year, the uncle led a total of 119 to believe in Jesus. He had been the chairman of the local Buddhist temple; but now he is a person of peace with 100-fold multiplication!

Hallelujah!

going to the Father." When the Lord Jesus ascended to our Heavenly Father, our Father gave us the Holy Spirit.

The disciples followed Jesus for three and a half years; they had Kingdom knowledge, but no power. When Jesus came to the region of Caesarea Philippi, he asked his disciples, "Who do people say the Son of Man is?"

They replied, "Some say John the Baptist; others say Elijah; and still others, Jeremiah or one of the prophets."

"But what about you?" he asked. "Who do you say I am?" Simon Peter answered, "You are the Messiah, the Son of the living God."

Jesus replied, "Blessed are you, Simon son of Jonah, for this was not revealed to you by flesh and blood, but by my Father in heaven."

From that time on Jesus began to explain to his disciples that he must go to Jerusalem and suffer many things at the hands of the elders, the chief priests and the teachers of the law, and that he must be killed and on the third day be raised to life.

Peter took him aside and began to rebuke him. "Never, Lord!" he said. "This shall never happen to you!"

Jesus turned and said to Peter, "Get behind me, Satan! You are a stumbling block to me; you do not have in mind the concerns of God, but merely human concerns" (Matthew 16:13-17:23).

Here, Jesus was not calling Peter Satan; but Jesus was ordering Satan to retreat from Peter's heart and stand behind him. It was necessary for Jesus to stand between Peter and Satan to protect Peter.

When Jesus left the disciples through his death on the cross, they were all scattered and lost. When Jesus was crucified, they failed; even Peter denied the Lord three times. Even when Jesus had risen from the dead, the disciples hid together afraid, with all the doors and windows closed.

Jesus had to enter among them and give them peace. He continued with them until the last day when Jesus was ascending to heaven. More than 500 persons were gathered in the Mount of

Olives and they asked him, "Lord, are you at this time going to restore the Kingdom to Israel?"

Instead Jesus gave them a new commandment: "Do not leave Jerusalem, but wait for the gift my Father promised, which you have heard me speak about. For John baptized with water, but in a few days you will be baptized with the Holy Spirit....But you will receive power when the Holy Spirit comes on you; and you will be my witnesses in Jerusalem, and in all Judea and Samaria, and to the ends of the earth" (Acts 1:6; 4-5, 8).

This is the important final commandment that Jesus gave to his disciples before his ascension into heaven after having already given his Great Commission. The Great Commission in Matthew was to share the gospel with everyone and make them all disciples (trainers).

But in this final command, Jesus told them to be baptized with the Holy Spirit, filled with the Holy Spirit. This is the only power that gives us the ability to share the gospel and train others to become disciples. Jesus began with a Great Commission, a proclamation, followed by the way to achieve that mission.

Jesus's strategy is perfect; he does not just order us to go, but gives us the power to go! Many Christians say, "I understand and I am willing, but I cannot do it." Of course the Father knows that we cannot do it. That is why he gave us the Holy Spirit. The Holy Spirit gives us the power that we need, and with that power, we are able to do what was impossible before!

## THE COMING OF THE HOLY SPIRIT

This time they listened carefully. After returning to Jerusalem, 120 persons in Mark's upper room spent time in urgent prayer until Pentecost. "Suddenly a sound like the blowing of a violent wind came from heaven and filled the whole house where they were sitting. They saw what seemed to be tongues of fire that separated and came to rest on each of them. All of them were filled with the Holy Spirit and began to speak in other tongues as the Spirit enabled them" (Acts 2:2-4). Because this sounded like an earthquake, many people of the city gathered to see what was happening.

Now that the disciples were filled with the Holy Spirit, they instantly had the ability and their reactions were different. They no longer said, "Close the door and windows!" The Bible tells us that Peter and the other Apostles stood up and preached the gospel boldly.

Praise the Lord! On that day, 3,000 people decided to believe in Jesus. On another day, Peter and John healed a lame man at the Temple gate, called Beautiful, and on that day, 5,000 men believed in Jesus. Yes, as soon as the disciples were filled with the Holy Spirit, they had powerful ability in Christ. They were able to do many miracles, as Jesus did. They were able to lead many to believe in the Lord and even raise the dead.

Jesus did not leave Palestine all his life, but today every Christian is filled with the Spirit of Jesus. From different corners of the world at the same time, we are able to bring the lost to Christ and also show miracles and wonders wherever we go. This is more than what Jesus did when he was alive!

When the Messiah was on earth, the disciples were with Jesus every day, listened to his teachings daily, and often saw his miracles. However, Jesus is Jesus; the disciples are disciples. The physical Jesus could not enter into the flesh of the disciples.

This all changed when Jesus rose from the dead. After the ascension, the Father sent the Holy Spirit and the Spirit of the Lord filled the disciples. After being baptized in the Holy Spirit, that Spirit of the Lord dwelt in the hearts of the disciples. The disciples were very different after they were filled with the Holy Spirit.

The Holy Spirit changed how the disciples functioned. In the Old Testament, when people were deciding on an issue or electing a person, they did not know how to decide or choose. So they would cast lots to decide before God. Even while they were waiting for the Pentecost event, the disciples decided to choose a replacement for Judas by casting lots to choose Matthias. Because they were not yet filled with the Holy Spirit, they only knew to let God decide through casting lots. But after the Holy Spirit came, everyone who followed the Lord was filled with the Holy Spirit, and with the Holy Spirit in every believer's heart, everything was different. Later, when the church elected the seven deacons, they no longer decided by casting lots. They voted in an election. This was because the Holy Spirit was in their hearts moving them to know God's choice.

Today in a church or organization, when we make a decision regarding the selection of pastors, elders, or deacons or any other decision, we vote rather than draw lots. Why then do we sometimes make the wrong decision, i.e. we elect the wrong person? This is because individuals in the congregation claim to be Christians, but unfortunately not every person who is a believer lets the Holy Spirit fill their hearts.

I often think of the name "Jesus Christ." Jesus is the name of the Son of God, and none of us can be Jesus, but each of us who believe in him can be filled with the Spirit of Jesus Christ. After being filled with the Spirit of Jesus, each of us becomes "a little Christ."

We all know that the term "Christian" comes from the Church of Antioch. It was not the believers in Antioch who called themselves Christians, but people outside the church. They saw these people in the church at Antioch, their lives, their behavior, their words and deeds were very much like those of Jesus Christ, so they called these believers "Christ's people"! Christians" are "Christ people" which are the source of the term Christian. Because they have the Spirit of Christ in their heart, they are "Christians," aka "Christ people" or "little Christs"!

So it is not that we call ourselves "Christians." When one is with the Lord, they must have the Spirit of Christ in their heart and be truly filled with the Spirit. Their every move should reflect the essence of Jesus Christ, so that others naturally recognize that they are "Christians."

## BAPTISM OF THE HOLY SPIRIT

But what we are going to show here is that the Holy Spirit (being touched by the Holy Spirit) and the baptism of the Holy Spirit (being filled with the Holy Spirit) are two different things.

Every believer must first be touched by the Holy Spirit in order to recognize Jesus as Lord, to accept that Jesus is Lord. But that is only the initial life of the believer. Yes, when you accept the Lord there is joy and peace, but you do not yet have the ability to work.

After the resurrection, during a meeting of the disciples, Jesus breathed on them and said, "Receive the Holy Spirit" (John 20:22).

The disciples had received the Holy Spirit, but still had no ability, and did not share the gospel. Soon after, they went back to their old line of work as fishermen until the Lord ascended to heaven when they were given another important order – to wait for the filling of the Holy Spirit!

After they were filled with the Holy Spirit they truly were given ability and power. As Ezekiel has written, "I will give them an undivided heart and put a new spirit in them; I will remove from them their heart of stone and give them a heart of flesh" (Ezekiel 11:19).

As God's Spirit fills us, we can then have this Spirit speak to us as God says in Ezekiel 36:27, "And I will put my Spirit in you and move you to follow my decrees and be careful to keep my laws." So we believe in the Lord because we are moved by the Holy Spirit. To live the Christian "life of Christ," we must be filled with the Holy Spirit. But how can we be filled with the Holy Spirit? The answer is through prayer! The Bible says pray and wait, then you will receive. So the life of prayer is the most important thing in the life of a Christian. The most important thing we train our trainers to do every day is to pray.

## PRAYER LIFE

I grew up in a pastor's home, but I did not like to pray. When I was a child, while going to bed at night, my mother would remind me, "Ying, you have not prayed all day today. How can you sleep? You must pray first before you can sleep."

Because I did not want to pray, I told her I didn't know how. My mom taught me to memorize a standard children's prayer. Every night when I went to sleep, I would look back at my mother and see her looking at me. I knew that I could not escape, so I kneeled down to pray. Even now, I know that prayer like the back of my hand.

"Thank the Father for giving me the grace of God, and giving me a healthy body every day. Now I ask the Father to forgive my sins; that I may do good with a good heart, and take me into heaven in the future. Let my family also believe in God. Hear my prayer in Jesus's name. Amen!"

This was a very good child's prayer, but it meant nothing to me. I only knew that once I finished this prayer, I could go to sleep. This was merely a routine.

When I got married, my wife, Grace, found out that I did not like to pray. We were studying together at the seminary. As a seminary student, I would study theology and gather great knowledge, but this was not a real spiritual journey. I had no desire to pray. Often when it came time to sleep at night, Grace would remind me, "Ying! You have not prayed today, why are you going to sleep already?"

Oh no! Here we go again... Fortunately, since she was not my mom, I could brush her off. I would respond, "Okay, I'll pray now," and lay on our bed to pray. Seeing this, Grace would say, "How can you be so impolite to God?"

I would respond, "You don't understand. With this position, my back is to the world and my face is to God. This is actually the best position for prayer!" Within two minutes of "prayer" I would fall asleep. Grace would wake me up and say, "How can you sleep and pray at the same time? That is very disrespectful to God!"

I would respond, "You don't understand again. Falling asleep while praying means I am sleeping in God's embrace! This is one of the greatest enjoyments we have with God so you should not wake me." Today I would like to apologize for this pitiful witness.

But thanks to the Father's love, he helped me learn to pray, enjoy prayer, and know the importance of prayer through my wife Grace. My wife helped me understand that prayer is not just memorizing routine prayers. It also isn't just repenting or asking for things I want. The most important thing about prayer is enjoying the blessing of being with God. It is the moment of praise and gratitude.

Grace reminded me that Enoch walked with God for 300 years every day. What were they saying and doing together every day? They were enjoying each other; Enoch was gaining power from God, and listening to God's will. It was the time to worship God personally. So I began practicing prayer and learning to praise, worship, and enjoy this time of prayer.

One day I was kneeling in prayer and crying out to God in a loud voice. Suddenly Grace came up to me and said, "Ying stop! Quit praying!" I thought it was very weird and said, "Before I was not praying and you wanted me to pray. Now I am praying with great feeling and you want me to stop. I don't get it, why?"

Grace said, "Your 'prayer' is not really a prayer. Prayer is not yelling at God telling him what you want, but asking him to show you what he wants." I didn't understand and said, "If I do not tell God what I want, how can I get it?"

## A New Mother Finds Deliverance

When I was serving at Hong Kong Baptist Hospital, we gave every new mother a small Bible. It would contain their baby's photo, their birth date and time, and was autographed by the superintendent of the maternity department.

Every mother who received such a Bible really liked it, especially since it included the baby's photos and an actual autograph from the superintendent. They found them very precious.

But one day, when a new mother received her Bible, she suddenly started trembling. Even the bed shook, which caused the chaplain on duty to become very scared.

He came running to my office and asked me if I knew what was happening. I said there must be some evil spirit in her, so I went up to the maternity ward. I immediately went to her room, stood next to her, and started praying for her to drive out the demons. When I prayed, she cried even louder; the whole ward could hear the noise. The more I prayed, the louder she cried.

Finally, the duty nurse came to me and said, "You cannot continue like this, the other patients are becoming very scared."

I was very disappointed and went back to my office. I wondered why I was unable to drive out the evil spirits? Suddenly, I understood. I had immediately run to her room to pray for her in an attempt to drive the evil spirits out. I had not kneeled down to pray for the power of God.

She responded, "No Ying, you have to understand our Heavenly Father is a wonderful, true God. He created the universe and continues to keep it operating. Everything is in the hands of the Father. The Father loves us and takes care of us. The Bible says he protects us as the apple of his eye. He has even counted the number of hairs we have. Today, everything is in the Father's will. If it is not the will of the Father, nothing will happen to us. Therefore, we pray that we will seek the will of the Father and pray according to his will, not according to our will."

## SPEAKING OUT GOD'S WILL

I have come to understand that prayer is a very valuable spiritual mystery. Prayer is to first understand the will of the Father and

---

I then started to pray, "In the name of Jesus Christ of Nazareth, [demons] leave now for you cannot do anything here."

Instead, I had gone by myself, relying on my own experience and on my own strength. It was not enough to cast out demons. So, I knelt down to pray. I also called my wife, Grace, and my mother-in-law to ask them to pray for me at the same time. I continued to pray and fast from noon until 1:30 in the afternoon.

Then, I went back to the ward to try again to cast out the demons. As I went to the ward, the other chaplains and I started singing:

"In the cross, in the cross,
be my glory ever,
till my raptured soul shall find
rest beyond the river."

I then started to pray, "In the name of Jesus Christ of Nazareth, [demons] leave now for you cannot do anything here."

Suddenly, I heard a pop sound and the young mother became quiet. The whole ward was then filled with a sense of calm and peace, a very joyful feeling. Then I asked the young mother to pick up the little Bible again. When she did, she saw her new baby's photos and she was very joyful and grateful.

She said, "Please help me, I want to believe in Jesus."

So we shared with her about Jesus, who has power over Satan, and she immediately believed in Jesus.

Praise God!

then to say what the will of the Father is. This is the true meaning of prayer. But why does the Bible say ask and you will receive, seek and you will find, knock and the door will be opened to you? Yes, we must ask, seek, and knock.

Opening the door may be the will of the Father, but you must first knock. Only after knocking will the Heavenly Father open the door for you. If you do not knock, the Heavenly Father will not open the door for you. Although opening the door is God's will, if you never knock, He would rather not open the door until you knock.

Because God loves us, he wants us to work with him. He wants us to be co-workers. But the biggest question is how do we know the Heavenly Father will open the door for me, and knock on the door? This is the will of the Father. Then the question is what is the Father's will? How do we understand the Father's will? It comes down to seeking God as a prerequisite for these conditions.

Jesus said, "What is the price of two sparrows--one copper coin? What is the price of five sparrows—two copper coins? But not a single sparrow can fall to the ground without your Father knowing it" (Matthew 10:29a; Luke 12:6; Matthew 10:29b).

As you can see the fifth sparrow is free with the purchase of four. From here we know that even sparrows that are "free" would not fall to the ground unless it is the Father's will. Therefore all things are in accordance with God's will. We must seek the Father's will and pray according to his will. Praying is about saying what God's will is, so that his will is unimpeded in in our lives and in the world.

How do we seek out God's will? The answer – to offer ourselves! In Romans 12:1-2 Paul says: "Therefore, I urge you, brothers and sisters, in view of God's mercy, to offer your bodies as a living sacrifice, holy and pleasing to God—this is your true and proper worship. Do not conform to the pattern of this world, but be transformed by the renewing of your mind. Then you will be able to test and approve what God's will is—his good, pleasing and perfect will."

If we are to understand God's will, we must first offer ourselves to him. How do we offer ourselves? In the Old Testament, if you wanted to offer a bull to God as an offering, you must kill the animal and give it as a burnt offering to God – burn the body completely.

However, if you are reluctant to offer it all, and just cut off the ears or tail of the bull to offer to God, your neighbors would only hear the bull's screams of pain. This is most definitely not a complete offering to God. God would not accept this offering.

Today many people say they are giving themselves to God, but they are not really offering themselves totally to him. Others may hear them on their knees crying out to God, but this does not mean they are totally giving themselves to his will. Giving yourself completely to God means to fall facedown in front of him and relinquish all control to him.

When Ezekiel saw the full glory of God, he fell facedown before him and the Holy Spirit enabled him to stand up again. His life changed, becoming a holy, focused person for God's service. Ezekiel was completely changed and under the control of God (Ezekiel 3:23, 27).

Saul, on the road to Damascus, saw the glory of the Lord. His whole party immediately fell to the ground, and Saul rose as Paul the apostle to the Gentiles (Acts 9). John was on Patmos Island when he had a vision of the glory of the Lord, he immediately fell to the ground. When he stood up again, he became an apostle filled with love (Revelation 1).

Within our lives there will at least be one time when we should fall facedown at the feet of God. At that time, we must let our Lord come completely against our selfish desires. Only then will we be able to completely offer ourselves to him. We will be able to hear, test, and understand his will. When we hear the Father's will clearly, we should humbly and sincerely ask through prayer that the will of the Father be accomplished.

Let's look at Elijah's example. After three years of drought, the Lord told Elijah, "I will send rain on the land" (1 Kings 18:1). After Elijah won the battle on Mount Carmel and killed all the prophets of Baal, he could have sat down and waited for the rain to come from God. But that was not what he did.

The Bible tells us Elijah climbed to the top of Mount Carmel, kneeled down with his face between his knees and humbly prayed for the Lord to send rain. At first, I could not understand. God was the one who told Elijah he would send rain on the land. Now that Elijah had won the battle and killed the prophets of Baal, shouldn't God send the rain now? Why was it necessary for Elijah to humbly kneel down and beg for rain? It wasn't until later that I understood and learned from Elijah. He was truly one who was close to God and one who understood God's will.

**First**, God wants to work through us. He does not want to work alone, He wants us to work with him.

**Secondly**, God wanted Israel to see that once his servant, Elijah, asked him for rain, he immediately answered the prayer and sent rain. The Israelites did not understand the mystery of God. God first told Elijah it was going to rain, and this was what enabled Elijah to pray for rain. Therefore God's will came first, the prayer came after.

**Third**, now that we understand it is God's will, we have faith. We continue to pray until God's will is fulfilled, never giving up in our prayer life.

**Fourth**, we must humbly, confidently, patiently, and carefully look for the fulfillment of God's will. Each time Elijah prayed, he asked his servant to look for the results. This is responsible prayer. How long did Elijah humbly pray? How many times? Not once, not twice, but seven times all together!

Why do we usually pray once, twice, then give up on the third time? Elijah, knowing this was God's will, did not give up until God answered his prayer.

Another very important point is that after each time Elijah prayed, he wanted his servant to see the results. The fulfillment of the purpose of God through confirmation is indispensable. When we offer ourselves, it is important to also examine what the will of God is during our prayers, when the results of his will are achieved, and how well our requests are taken care of by God.

## HUMBLE, FAITHFUL, AND PATIENT PRAYER

Once we understand the will of God, we must pray humbly, faithfully, and patiently. We should carefully check for the fulfilling of God's will during this process. We must also continue to listen to the voice of God. Many people after hearing one direction from God focus solely on that direction. However, we need to continue to carry out God's command.

For example, God first commanded Abraham to offer his only son Isaac as a burnt offering to him. Abraham demonstrated obedience (Genesis 22:2). Can you imagine his inner pain? Isaac was born to him when Abraham was 100 years old. Isaac was his only son and now he was offering this son. He took his boy and went on a three-day journey.

He must have been unbelievably sad and filled with doubt, but he continued on in the Lord's command, continuing to carefully listen to the voice of God. As he tied Isaac up, the second command came from God, "You cannot lay a hand on the boy. Do not do anything to him."

Abraham had a very obedient and sensitive heart, he obeyed God and continued to listen and be very sensitive to the will of God. You and I see this Bible story as easy to follow, but it was never easy for Abraham.

Today, when God tells us to do something, it is often difficult to obey. Still we force ourselves to obey his command with a heavy, sad heart. Unfortunately if we continue to try and serve him without a sensitive, listening heart, it would not be true obedience. We can start thinking we have made a mistake and didn't hear him clearly. We can even miss the ongoing direction from God (the second, third and fourth commands of God) and not fully understand God's will. We can end up blaming God. That is really wrong!

Here is a final point that we should consider: when we clearly hear the will of God, we should not continue to try and bargain with God. In Numbers 22:6, King Balak asked the prophet Balaam to curse Israel. Balaam asked God, and from the beginning God told him not to go with them. But Balaam desired money and wealth, so he came back again and again to ask God if he could go. God finally let him go, but he was eventually met with a fatal disaster.

Today, many times we do the same thing, because we do not agree with God's will we return to God and try to bargain - this is something that should never be done.

The true meaning of prayer is working together with God according to his will:

1.  We must offer ourselves totally to him in total obedience. Fall before the face of God and let God break down the old me.

2.  Listen to and understand the will of God.

3.  Humbly pray and work together with God so that the will of God can flow through us without hindrance.

4.  Be patient, have confidence, and never give up seeking.

5.  Carefully examine how to fulfill God's will.

6.  With sensitivity continue to listen to the voice of God.

7.  Only with sincere prayer will the Holy Spirit fill us up so that we can complete the Lord's mission.

## DAILY PRAYER LIFE

We encourage our trainers to engage in a daily prayer life that should include at least the following four aspects:

## 1. THE BLOOD OF JESUS

In the heat of spiritual battle, we can ask our Father in heaven to send guardian angels to protect us. Ask the Father for complete filling of the Holy Spirit. Throughout our everyday life, there are many temptations from Satan to lure and attack us, so every day we need to seek the blood of Jesus to cover us. In this way we are following the path of the saints who came before us, about whom it was written, "They overcame him (Satan) by the blood of the Lamb, and by the word of their testimony...."(Revelation 12:11).

## 2. THE FULL ARMOR OF GOD

As we are fighting a spiritual battle, we must wear armor to fight the enemy. However, we cannot put it on just by talking about it. It must be done piece by piece.

Put on the Helmet of Salvation – one of the best gifts the Heavenly Father gives us is our imagination. Because of our imagination, we were able to have inventions such as the light bulb, telephone, computer, etc. But Satan also uses this gift of imagination to tempt us into committing a multitude of sins. We really have to be careful to daily put on the Helmet of Salvation.

Wear the Breastplate of Righteousness – today in many families and many churches there is conflict. This is because everyone seems to have their own ideas about what is right and what is wrong. When another person's worldview or moral code is not in accordance with my views of righteousness, then we think they are just wrong. In fact, none of us are perfect, and today I'm not asking you to be empathetic or compromise. I am not asking you to give up your heartfelt values, but today everyone must be concentric/inclusive in accordance with the heart of Jesus. The heart of Jesus is full of love, compassion, gentleness, humility and sacrifice.

Strap on the Belt of Truth – The truth is the Bible, the Word of God. We need to keep the Word of God in our hearts, just as we need to tighten our belt. We tighten our belts, because it makes us more powerful. We are then able to stand firmly on the basis of the victory that Jesus has for us and never fall.

Wear Shoes to bring the Good News of Peace – We have to be a person of peace wherever we go, spreading the Lord's love anywhere he sends us and at all times.

Hold the Shield of Faith – faith extinguishes the fiery arrows of the Evil One. Yes, even though we are weak, our Lord is a faithful God. His faithfulness and virtue protects us from all the attacks of Satan. Temptation, damage, destruction, backbiting, and envy are all banished by the shield of our faith in Christ. Praise the Lord!

Each of the above are defensive armor. There is only one offensive weapon, the Sword of the Spirit – God's holy word. Every time Satan wants to attack us, we should immediately, by the Holy Spirit's power, use the Word of God to repel the attack of the Evil One. Then we will be able to overcome it.

Jesus was also tempted three times. But three times he repulsed Satan with the Word of God. So we encourage our trainers to keep

God's Word in their hearts so that we can always have a sword available. In many areas, the police may at any time confiscate your cell phone, computer, and Bible. But if you put God's Word in your head, no one can confiscate it and you'll have a sword at your disposal.

## 3. ASK OUR HEAVENLY FATHER

According to the will of the Holy Spirit, God gives us every gift we need for ministry. For example, the fact that I can stand here today and share a message is a most precious gift to me.

As a child, I had stuttering problems. In many situations, I was unable to get out even one word. No one talked to me. I had no friends. It wasn't until I was in junior high school, during one weekend at a church's student fellowship group I was attending, the youth leader said to me, "Ying, during our fellowship next week, it will be your turn to read the devotional thought. It is only one page long."

I looked at him and shook my head no, but he said, "I believe you can. It's just one minute of reading, give it a try!" I really wanted to try, so when I got home I did vocal exercises and tried to read the page out loud. I practiced for a whole afternoon, and try as I might, I could not read a complete sentence. It broke my heart – I was so angry and disappointed. That night before going to bed, I put my Bible on the ground and kneeled on the Bible. I begged our Heavenly Father, "Please give me this gift to talk to others. By your grace I want the ability to speak fluently – just to share your word. Please help me!" I prayed every night, but I didn't make any progress.

Sadly, I headed to public school on Saturday morning as usual. One day a different teacher came into our classroom and stood directly in front of my desk. He said to me, "I know you have a stuttering problem and you cannot read fluently. I am a speech specialist and I can help you." Then he asked me to open my workbook. He pulled out a red pen and in my book he wrote in big letters the word "Slow." He said, "This is a very simple thing to correct. As you work through the sentences, remember to take it slowly."

Then he taught me to read a word with elongated tone, then take a breath and read the second word, and then exhale to relax. "Read slowly one word after another," he said, "You see, you are not stopping in progress through the sentence. It is very slow, but you can slowly accelerate. Soon, you will read much better."

That whole afternoon I used this method to practice reading out loud for the church student meeting that evening. At the youth fellowship that night, when it was my turn, I stood up and word-by-word slowly read the entire passage in the devotional. It was the first time I had ever done that in my life. Everyone clapped and encouraged me. This was such a wonderful gift from God!

Thanks be to our Heavenly Father! Even now I still have a nervous stammer sometimes when I speak. The good news is that the Lord's grace is sufficient for me to use even my stutter for his glory! If you are determined to serve God, pray and he will give you the appropriate gifts and abilities according to this promise.

## 4. THANKSGIVING FOR EVERYTHING

As I shared before, I had trouble speaking clearly starting at a young age. Over the years, people often misunderstood me, so I had a bad temper. I was quick to anger and did not deal well with my anger, especially during times of stress.

When we first got married, Grace found out she had a husband that would blow up at the slightest things. I was always sorry to disappoint her. Every time I would lose my temper, I would be eaten up with self-blame. I would kneel in prayer and plead with God about my guilt and punish myself, but things did not change. Again and again I would lose my temper, and it seemed that I had no control over it. I regretted my behavior, but could not change. Life was very painful.

While we were studying at seminary, Grace and I had different majors so our classes were often different. One day after school, I came home and opened the door. Grace looked at me and said, "Ying, today I have learned a new lesson. I am going to endlessly praise the Lord for your bad temper!" I was very surprised! "How can you praise God for my bad temper? We can thank the Lord for blessings, but how can we praise him for bad things?"

Grace showed me Psalm 22:3, "Yet you are enthroned as the Holy One; you are the one Israel praises." (Or "Yet you are holy, / enthroned on the praises of Israel.") She said, "If you praise God for everything, from your heart, he will come and live in your heart. He will make your life his precious throne to take full control of your life."

She explained to me some wonderful Bible truths, The Bible encourages us to "give thanks in all things," all is according to our Heavenly Father's will – both good and bad. He protects even the smallest components of our eyes and knows the number of the hairs on our head. If it were not the will of God, nothing would happen to us. As we lift up our praises and thanks to God, it honors the sovereignty of God. We believe God sustains everything.

Do you remember when Paul and Silas were in prison? They did not complain. Late into the night, they sang praises to God in prayer. The result was a great earthquake, a miracle happened, and they led the jailer's family to the Lord!

When King Jehoshaphat was besieged by an enemy army, he was afraid. He led the people to go to the temple to pray. As they finished their prayer, they raised their voices to praise the glory of God. The king then opened the gates and the choir went before the Israelite army praising the Lord. As they praised the almighty God, God fought for them and gave them a great victory (2 Chronicles 20:1-30)! Grace then said to me, "Please join me in praising God for your bad temper which you cannot change. Let's acknowledge his sovereignty and let him rule our lives!"

At that time I was 27 years old; for the first time in my life I knelt down with my wife and praised God for my bad temper. I totally surrendered to God. I was profoundly grateful to him and praised our Father from my heart. I was too weak and could not manage on my own, but thanks be to God for his tolerance and love for me. I thanked the Father for accepting the old me that I could not control. From that time on, I learned to praise and do thanksgiving "homework" every day.

Some time later, Grace said to me, "Ying! I have been looking at our monthly calendar. Over the past few months, you've changed a lot. Every day since we got married, I marked each time you lost your temper. Some days it was three times a day, some days it was five times a day." How terrible I used to be! For months, she looked at the calendar every day, prayed for me and thanked the Lord for me. I was so ashamed. However, I truly and deeply praise our Heavenly Father's great love! He saved me and healed me. Since then, I have been full of gratitude and praise for this testimony in our lives! At all times, we encourage our trainers to thank and to praise God as they live their lives in front of others.

## Discussion Questions

- Do you have the Holy Spirit working with you?

- What is the difference between receiving the Holy Spirit and being baptized with the Holy Spirit?

- What is the meaning of prayer?

- How can we understand our Heavenly Father's will?

- What attitude should we have in prayer?

# 5

## The Joy of the Christian Life

A Holy Spirit-filled person will have a heart that cares for others. As they see those around them, their hearts will raise a strong voice calling: this person or that person needs salvation! So we must all have our testimony prepared in order to share the love of Jesus with those around us.

## PERSONAL SALVATION TESTIMONY

Write down your testimony. It is best to write it in a story form that includes three parts:

1. Before finding Christ, what kind of person were you? What were your behavior and thoughts like? For example, were you a person who never experienced peace? Did you have a short temper? Write down your original frame of mind.

2. Under what circumstances did you come to believe in Jesus?

3. After you put your trust in Christ, what life changes have you experienced? Have you experienced the peace and joy of life?

Your story should not be too long. People these days are very busy and do not have the time to listen to a long story. A one-minute story will give you the chance to share your story with anyone at any place. As long as people have the opportunity to listen, they have the opportunity to believe in Jesus.

You do not need to wait until you find people with whom to share your story. You can immediately share your story on the Internet in avenues such as Facebook and Twitter or even through e-mail and text messages. You will probably be met with unexpected results. Many people will respond to you giving you the opportunity to train them.

## A Little Girl Who Rose Again

When I was a hospital chaplain, I used to pray for each surgery from inside the operating room. One day I was called in to pray for a little girl who was badly injured in a car accident and had a blood clot in her brain. Half way through the operation, the anesthesiologist told the surgeon that the little girl showed no signs of life. The surgeon wondered if he should continue.

He turned to me and said, "Pastor, please pray for me. This is a very difficult surgery to perform and the procedure is very costly. I must discuss with her parents and see what they want to do."

We went to the waiting room to tell the little girl's father and mother. The parents said, "Pastor, please pray for us. We want the doctor to complete the surgery."

The surgeon returned to the operating room to complete the little girl's surgery. He carefully removed the clot from the little girl's brain. After the procedure was completed, as the medical staff turned the little girl over, she suddenly began to breathe again and her blood pressure returned to normal.

This was a miracle! After three months of rehabilitation, she completely recovered and was discharged from the hospital. Through this experience, her whole extended family came to believe in Jesus.

Thank God!

## NAME LIST

Remember, there are really only two kinds of people in the world: the lost and the saved. So to begin, first list the names of all of your unsaved relatives and friends.

Pray quietly so that you may think of the list of names of all unsaved family members, relatives, friends, classmates, colleagues, and neighbors. Also list those who you think are far away from our Heavenly Father. Once you complete your list, pray for them daily; do not only mention their names in prayer, but lift them up to the Lord in detail one by one.

For example, in your prayer for a brother you have, you would talk about where your brother currently is; what he is doing; what situations he is facing; why you're concerned about him. We want to ask the Holy Spirit to move his heart and give him a heart that hungers for the truth. At the same time, pray for yourself that the Lord will give you the opportunity, wisdom, love, and the words to use while you share the gospel.

Split your names into groups of five. Group A will consist of the five the Lord wants you to share with immediately. Group B will consist of the next five you want to evangelize, then Group C, D, E, etc. Share with at least five people each week. Pray for them and the Holy Spirit will guide you so that you may lead them to salvation and they will become your trainees (disciples).

Now list the names of all of your Christian friends and relatives.

Once again, quietly pray and ask the Holy Spirit to help you write down the names of all your Christian friends and relatives. Pray for them daily that the Holy Spirit will prepare your heart and theirs for the training to come. Split the names into groups and encourage yourself to contact at least two to three people each week so that you may start to train them.

## THREE LEVELS OF JOY

Why do so many Christians lack the feeling of joy and fulfillment in their lives?

After becoming Christians many people only have a short period where they are very enthusiastic because it is a new experience for them. They may go to worship service every week, but do not experience true joy in their lives. This is because they are still fragile believers. As such not only do they need to build up themselves, they also need to help build up others in Christ. However, we have found that there is growing joy when we obey the Lord.

A Christian that leads another person to Christ will feel joy as even the angels in heaven will rejoice and be happy for them.

Christians should not only lead others to Christ; they must train others to form groups of disciples as they organize their own training groups. These training groups are emerging house churches, groups of people called together by the Lord to worship God and enjoy fellowship together with him. A house church, like at training group, is not limited by the number of people participating. These trainers will experience even deeper, satisfying joy. This is because they are not only members of the Kingdom, but are contributors to the Kingdom.

But Christians should not only organize their own small training groups, they must also train the members of their group to share the gospel and start their own small groups. This begins the next generation of believers and the next generation of small groups. Trainers who train others to make disciples will then begin to experience the deepest joy of the Christian life.

## Discussion Questions

- Write your story and name lists now.

- Have you ever experienced the joy that comes from God?

- When you have an opportunity, are you always ready to tell your story?

- Where have you shared your testimony?

- How should you pray for others?

# 6

## The Power of Simplicity

Simplicity is one of the keys to T4T success.

Over the years with the best of intentions, we thought of many different approaches to teach our church members what we know, evangelism methods that have worked for us, and even methods that we found were unsuccessful. However, none of them did anything with the knowledge. We later found out the reason was because it was all too complicated so they did not even know what to do with the knowledge nor how to implement the methods. Therefore, we simplified all the training material we had and made it easy to implement. Over time, we learned to only teach a small portion at a time so that each person would realize, "This is very simple – I can do it, and I will do it."

For example, if you taught someone 100 concepts all at once, they would think there is an abundance of different concepts. However, how would they realistically teach someone else all 100 concepts? It would be too difficult a task for them. On the other hand, if you were only to teach them three concepts at a time: 1-2-3 and they practice 1-2-3 immediately, the next day, they can easily teach others 1-2-3.

The next week they could return to learn 4-5-6 and practice 4-5-6. Then they could once again go and teach others 4-5-6. With

this simple process repeating, everyone is able to implement the
processes. Unfortunately, after many people learn T4T, they feel it
is too simple, and start adding a bit here and there, and unknow-
ingly make it complicated.

They then complain that T4T is an unsuccessful method. However, this is a matter of principle. Yes, your heart may be in the
right place and you want to give them the very best, just as King
Saul who wanted to give David his armor when David was going
out to face Goliath. Saul's armor was the finest and he wanted
to give David the best he had, but David was barely able to walk
with the armor on. David removed this heavy armor and defeated
Goliath with just a simple weapon – a stone and a sling. Saul had
the best of intentions in helping David, but the armor was just
too heavy for him.

Jesus said in Matthew 11:30: "For my yoke is easy and my burden is light." Yes, you may have good intentions, but if you teach
too much and it is too complicated, then no one will be able to
understand and implement it.

It is also important to remember the witness of a very well
educated individual, the Apostle Paul. In 1 Corinthians 2:1-5, Paul
wrote:

> And so it was with me, brothers and sisters. When I came to you, I did not
> come with eloquence or human wisdom as I proclaimed to you the testi-
> mony about God. For I resolved to know nothing while I was with you ex-
> cept Jesus Christ and him crucified. I came to you in weakness with great
> fear and trembling. My message and my preaching were not with wise
> and persuasive words, but with a demonstration of the Spirit's power,
> so that your faith might not rest on human wisdom, but on God's power.

Keeping a simple approach is truly one of the key reasons T4T
is successful. There may be those that think the first six lessons
are too short and simple and would add a little here and there.
This results in the lessons becoming very long and complicated.
When that happens, not only will new believers not be able to
teach others the same lessons, but even mature believers won't
be able to do it.

There are also some who consider the seventh lesson having
only three questions to be too simple and not an enjoyable Bible

study. As such, they add many questions so that there would be a lot more discussions.

Yes, many people like to have discussion. However, too much discussion leads to no action. Intellectuals are especially attracted to having deep discussions. But what about next steps? Does your trainee have the same faith and abilities to teach the same way, to start the same discussions in their small groups? This may be too difficult. It is very easy to make a training complicated. To simplify a complicated training so that anyone can implement it and would want to implement it is completely different. The secret of T4T's success is to keep it simple, so that anyone can utilize it and everyone will want to utilize it. It is not considered a success until you get to that point.

## Discussion Questions

• What is simple? What is complex?

• Are there any changes you should make to your former training material and method?

• What, if any, are the differences between your former training method and what you have just learned?

# 7

## Seven-Lesson Discipleship

When a baby first receives life, its immediate need is to breathe. Once the baby starts breathing, it needs food. Next this new child will need a good family to take care of it. This child will then come to recognize who the head of the household is and accept parental love and discipline. After growing up, the young adult will become a productive member of society and work to give back to its family.

This young adult can then live a good, healthy life with healthy habits, regular exercise, and eating healthy food. In this way the person will grow up to be a well-balanced adult. We follow the same pattern in our simple course lessons. Once again, I would like to remind you to keep things simple so that anyone is able to do it and everyone is willing to do it. Once things begin to get complicated, people start to put it off and not do it.

After you share your story with others, it is important to remember to share Jesus's story right away. The first lesson is the story of Jesus and his assurance of salvation. After listening to the story of Jesus and accepting him as their savior, they will be born again and gain salvation. Gaining this new life is the same as a newborn baby receiving their life.

When they return the next week, it is time to teach them the second lesson: understanding prayer. Prayer is like breathing for the Christian life. Humans need to breathe at all times of the day or they will die. Similarly, Christians should pray at any time, place, and situation otherwise it is impossible to live out Christ in us. So it is very important to teach a new believer to have a strong prayer life.

The third lesson is daily devotions. A daily need for a baby is the care of their parents. Similarly new believers need daily intimate moments with our Heavenly Father. Regardless of how busy one is, it is important to find a time to talk with God alone every day. Since this is a time of personal worship with God, it is important to find a quiet place so that you may commune with him. In this lesson we help them set up a daily Bible reading plan; we encourage all our trainees to read three chapters from the Old Testament and one chapter from the New Testament each day. In this way, they will finish reading the entire Bible in one year.

Prayer is where you talk to the Lord. Reading the Bible is where the Lord speaks to you. This is a very important process. Many people never hear God speak to them and some of them just don't want to hear. Without ever putting the Word of God in their hearts, how will they be able to hear God speak to them?

The fourth lesson is the church gathering. The church is a family so we call each other brothers and sisters. This new baby needs a good family to take care of him. Even without a house, a family is still a family. Similarly, a church is not based on a building. Even if the church gathering does not have a building, a church is still a church. The most important part is for a church to follow the patterns that Jesus gave us: worship, fellowship, training, evangelism, and the power of the Holy Spirit. In addition, as Jesus taught us, the church must observe the Lord's Supper, baptism, and offerings.

The fifth lesson is that God is our Heavenly Father. The child must respect and obey his parents. In the same way, we must teach those who are born again to recognize their Heavenly Father and respect and obey him. Our Father loves us with an everlasting love. He gave his only begotten Son, who died on the cross for our sins. If we believe in Jesus and accept him as our Savior, we inherit the identity of being children of God. Through his love, he provides us with all we need. If you want to serve God, he will provide you with all that you need including spiritual gifts. Through his love, he protects us. During any day, we may be faced with difficulties, dangers, or attacks but he will protect us. Through his love he disciplines us. "Those whom I love I rebuke and discipline" (Revelation 3:19). We truly live in the love of our Heavenly Father.

The sixth lesson is spreading the gospel. After children grow up, they should give back and also go to work. Starting from the first lesson, we encourage new believers to immediately evangelize. However, some may resist and not go. Therefore, at this time we once again call to them. Everyone needs to hear the four calls emanating from God's creation: from above, from below, from inside of us, and from outside. Everyone should respond to these calls to "Go!" and share the gospel.

The four calls are motivations for sharing the gospel that we use in vision casting for our trainees. These four calls from God come from above (Isaiah 6:1-8, "Whom shall I send, and who will go for us?"), from below (Luke 16:27-28, " I beg you, father, send Lazarus to my father's house..."), from inside of us (1 Corinthians 9:16-17, " Woe to me if I do not preach the gospel!"), and from outside of us (Acts 16:9, "Come over to Macedonia and help us."). These calls are further addressed in Appendix, Lesson 6.

The seventh lesson is participatory Bible study. Once a new believer understands and begins acting on the basic truth, we should immediately teach them the most important link in the chain for leading and establishing small groups – a long term, simple Bible study method.

Every time you preach or exegete a passage of the Bible for them, they are able to accept and learn from it. However, this leaves believers with a dependence on you and your teaching. They do not yet know how to receive God's light, grace, and blessings for themselves. Therefore, we must teach them a simple Bible study method. In this way they will not only be able to study the Bible for themselves to build themselves up, they will also be able to lead small groups in studying the Bible, and teach those members to study the Bible for themselves.

There are many spiritual resources and materials for studying the Bible. However, most new believers are unable to help teach others how to study the Bible for themselves or understand the truths Jesus wants us to obey.

The fact is reference books and Bible study materials are no replacement for the Word of God. The Bible is the best resource for helping a person to learn and receive strength to trust and obey the Lord's words. This is a very important lesson. We need to ask the Holy Spirit to shine upon us and guide us so that we may grow spiritually. Starting from the seventh lesson, the Bible is T4T's only discipleship material. To grow in Christ, we train our disciples to read several Bible verses at one time and answer three simple questions. We can remember these three questions with the acronym S-O-S.

1. First, what does this passage "say"? Everyone can take turns sharing the passage in their own words. Once you put it in your own words, it becomes much easier to remember and understand what the Scripture says.

2. Second, what does this passage teach us to "obey"? The true significance of Bible study is to obey the Word of the Lord.

3. Finally, what should we "share" with others from this passage? We learn the Bible, not just for knowledge, but to share with others.

This is a simple S-O-S method of Bible study that we must not complicate. If we start complicating it, most people are unable to remember it. You can imagine, in the long-term this will be a very detailed Bible study method. Some people think that the three questions are too simple so they add a number of other questions. In this way, they think they are enriching the discussion and adding depth. However, complex methods for many people (including new believers) are too difficult to teach to someone else.

T4T reinforces the importance of the Bible in the life of new believers and trainers in both Lesson 3 (daily devotions) and Lesson 7 (long-term Bible study). Lesson 3 teaches them to have a daily Bible reading, reading four chapters of the Bible each day. Lesson 7 teaches them to have long-term Bible study, paving the way for in-depth, comprehensive Bible knowledge and understanding.

You will find these seven lessons in the Appendix in the back of this book.

## Discussion Questions

- How will you teach these lessons?

- Are your trainers understanding what you are teaching? Are they able to teach it to others?

- Do you think these lessons are too simple?

- Are you able to teach this material without looking at it?

# 8

# The T4T Process

T4T is more than an event; it is a process that grows into a lifestyle.

During each of our trainings, we utilize the three one-thirds process. This is essentially dividing our time into three parts of roughly equal length of time.

**Part One: Praise and worship, pastoral care, accountability, and vision casting.**

**Part Two: Today's lesson, a simple Bible study.**

**Part Three: Practice, set goals, and pray with each other.**

There are eight indispensable activities that take place in this three-part process. In every meeting, we always start with praise and worship to the Lord. We then move on to greeting one another, caring for one another, and praying for one another. We always pay our respects to God first, then to one another.

Accountability includes supporting one another, exhorting each other, and reviewing what each person did in the past week. This includes sharing with one another, for example, "In the past week, how many people did I share the gospel with? What were the results? How many small groups did I train? Are there any testimonies or challenges to share?"

Remember, it is important to share both successes and failures so that we can help one another. We can model for one another our successes, and learn from one another through the challenges we experience. This opening portion of the weekly meeting is a precious time for the small group as it is the time each person within the group uses love to mutually exhort, encourage, and share their successful methods and challenges with the whole group.

This is one of the most important periods within the training. At the end of this opening period, it is important for the training leader to give the trainees a weekly vision casting to remind them of Jesus's Great Commission. In the vision-casting portion, the trainer encourages the trainees by reminding them of the Heavenly Father's heart, or the power of the Holy Spirit, or the importance of listening to the four callings, or the character of the Kingdom worker.

The second third is today's lesson. Starting with Lesson 1 in the first week to Lesson 6 on the sixth week. The seventh lesson starts long-term inductive Bible study (S.O.S.).

The last third begins with the trainee reviewing each part of the three-thirds meeting, and practicing the new lesson learned this week. This is the time for trainees to get familiar with this lesson so that you may teach this same lesson to others starting the next day. Then, it is time to set your goals: "How many people will I be sharing with in this week? How many small groups will I be training? Who do I need to pray for?" We often break into groups of two to three people to discuss our goals for the following week and support each other through prayer. In this way, we are better equipped to exhort one another during next week's accountability time.

For example, you will be able to ask questions such as, "I remembered we prayed for the five friends you were going to share the gospel with. How did that go?" It is because we set goals that we can be accountable for them. We can also pray about the new goals we have set. Furthermore, we can ask one another how the goals are progressing during anytime of the week via phone calls or text messages. This is the best method.

Using this training process, your trainees will not feel alone – they have others working alongside them. This also helps reinforce our feelings of responsibility for our small groups so that they may grow, reproduce, and multiply generation by generation. This is the best way. I urge you to follow this principle without getting off track – you will surely see results.

## STEP BY STEP

Let's take a moment to recap the steps involved in implementing T4T, step by step.

The first time you encourage trainers to obey the Great Commission, teach them to develop a name list. Then, have them split the name list into groups of five names each, and give time for them to pray for each name.

After this, have them write down their own testimonies and repeatedly practice telling their story so that they become very familiar with telling their story. Then teach them the first lesson – the story of Jesus – the assurance of Christ's salvation. After we share our own story with someone, they may be moved because of it. However, they still need to listen to the story of Jesus's plan of salvation, because they do not yet know Jesus and do not yet understand the truth. As such, it is important to introduce them to Jesus as soon as possible so that they may accept him. Once they have accepted Jesus, we also want them to repeatedly practice their own story, and teach them the first lesson so that they too can share and train others the next day.

It is important to distribute five copies of the first lesson and pray for each person you train during the first training. Then, encourage them to share their story and the story of Jesus with at least five other people within the following week. When they return the next week for their second training, have them share their results of sharing the gospel within the past week. At this time, they should also encourage and exhort each other.

Then you can teach them the second lesson and repeat the same three one-thirds process of the first training. Make sure to provide them with enough materials to train other new believers. Then, have those new believers write down their name lists and their testimonies. Using the same method, they can train the next generation of new believers who should be encouraged in the same way to train the next generation. Training generation to generation of new believers will lead to rapid church multiplication. We should know that new believers are often the most enthusiastic people to share the gospel. As such, we should trust them as our Lord trusts them (Mark 5:19-20).

We should not encourage them to bring others into our small group. We are training them to become a trainer (disciple). They must start and train their own small groups. It is not our desire to increase the number of people in our small groups but to have their training continue generation after generation. In this way we follow the T4T three-thirds training process to encourage, exhort, vision cast, provide adequate practice, set goals, and pray for one another.

We must never give up on anyone, nor blame anyone, but only give love and encouragement. Does our Heavenly Father not often support us? In our trainings, if there is someone who returns repeatedly without sharing the gospel, we would then encourage them personally. As part of this encouragement, we request them to take out their name list and share the situation of each person on their list. Then, we pray together for these people and stay in contact through daily texts and phone calls for continued encouragement.

## OVERVIEW OF THE T4T PROCESS

At the most basic level, to shepherd a church is to cultivate believers, training them to become disciples. Remember, true disciples are trainers. Therefore, the main purpose of everything we do is to move everyone towards becoming trainers, with rapid propagation down from one generation to another.

There are seven essentials in this process of cultivating disciples.

### 1. The Foundation

- Sharing the Word of God is the foundation (1 Corinthians 14:26; 1 Peter 4: 4-11).

- Fully trust God. Completely obey God (John 14:21; James 1:22).

- Constantly pray to God. Ask God for direction and help (Ephesians 6:18-20; Matthew 5:44; Luke 18:9-40; 1 Thessalonians 5:16-18).

- Follow in Jesus's footsteps every day; do not deviate. Regardless of language and behavior standards, establish all of your foundations on the Word of God (Acts 17:11; 1 Thessalonians 5:16-18).)

- In everything give thanks, because God is faithful (1 Thessalonians 5:24; 1 Corinthians 1:9; 10:13; 1 John 1:9).

## 2. The Worker

- Immediately put new believers in the Kingdom work of the gospel (2 Timothy 2:2).

- Train local people to become leaders (Titus 1:5-9; Acts 20: 16-17).

- Raise up persons of peace. If you share the gospel, then you are a person of peace (Acts 8:26-27; 10:21; Luke 10:1-9).

## 3. The Harvest

- The harvest field is all those around you who have not yet heard the gospel (Matthew 28:19-20; Acts 1:1-8).

- You should train all of the Christians around you to join in the harvest (Luke 10:2).

## 4. The Target

- The gospel of the Kingdom will be preached in all the world (Matthew 24:14; Acts 17:1-2; 22-27).

- Give special attention to places that have not yet heard the gospel (Romans 15:20).

- Your goal is that every person hears the Word of God (Acts 19:10).

- Continue to the ends of the earth (Acts 1:8).

## 5. The Development

- Every believer should develop their own training groups – this is the most rapid multiplication method (Acts 9:31; 16:1-5).

- Sow generously to reap generously (2 Corinthians 9:6; Hebrews 4:12).

## 6. The Method

- Pursue a church-multiplication strategy (Acts 9:31; 8:1, 4; and 19:10).

- Teach them in a small-group setting.

- Train and practice with them until they become true trainers.

- Every trainer, in all locations, is capable of immediately starting their own training group.

- A new small group church can immediately establish another small group or multiple small groups.

- Believe that God will personally lead his flock (1 Corinthians 2:5).

## 7. The Time

- The time is now. Do not wait (Luke 10:11-12; Romans 10:13-15)!

## ESTABLISH GOALS

Now that you have completed the basics of T4T, you have really only just begun. It is time now to set goals for how you will begin raising up disciples, trainers who will train others to multiply Christ's Kingdom. Let's begin with a goals list of persons with whom you will share, and persons you will train.

We need to pray and rely on the Lord's grace to help us achieve the goals you list. Set very clear numerical goals within the list. This list will help to encourage and remind us so that we may achieve these goals.

## 1. What is your goal for the next two weeks?

- What will you be doing in the next two weeks?
- Who will you be sharing the gospel with (your name list)?
- How many people will you be training? How many small groups?

## 2. What is your goal for the next 12 months?

- What are your plans for the next 12 months?
- How many trainers will you be training? Include the trainers being trained by your trainers – that is, the second, third, fourth, etc. generations of trainers.

Do not be anxious about anything, but in everything by prayer and supplication with thanksgiving let your requests be made known to God. And the peace of God, which surpasses all understanding, will guard your hearts and your minds in Christ Jesus. I can do all things through him who strengthens me (Philippians 4:6-7, 13).

## WORDS OF ENCOURAGEMENT

**Pray!**

**Keep it simple!**

**Don't doubt that you can do it – just do it!**

**Be strong and courageous!**

**Do your work!**

**Your Heavenly Father will be with you!**

## Discussion Questions

- How are you going to change your existing shepherding and training methods?

- What is the difference between this three-thirds process and how you were training?

- What do you think are the most important aspects?

- If you run out of time what do you do? Are there portions you can cut out?

- When are you planning to use this three-thirds process in your trainings?

- Which of these elements are most important to you?

- Are you ready to implement this process?

# 9

## Hidden Wisdom

This chapter was not written by Ying and Grace Kai, but rather by the book's editor who is both a long-time student and practitioner of T4T. It is not written without Ying's approval or agreement, but there are some things that it is easier for an outsider to write. There is much about T4T and its secrets to success that are better noted by an observer practitioner than by the authors themselves.

**1. The kind of person God uses.** Ying and Grace would never describe themselves as extraordinary. In fact, they would insist that T4T can be done by any follower of Jesus Christ; indeed, anyone can obey Christ's Great Commission. And yet when we examine the life of Ying and Grace, and every highly effective T4T practitioner, we see some common, yet extraordinary, characteristics.

Ying and Grace are persons of prayer, often spending hours in prayer each day. In addition to prayer for God's Holy Spirit power to fill, lead, and follow after them, their ministry is saturated in prayer. They pray for lost persons with whom to share their story. They pray for persons with whom they share that God would grant them the faith to say yes to the good news. They pray for those whom they train that God would empower them to be fruitful witnesses for Christ. Prayer is the atmosphere in which T4T movements emerge and thrive.

During a T4T training, I was once asked, "And how about you? Do you spend two hours a day in prayer?" I paused for a moment before responding, "Two hours a day is far from natural for me, or for any Christian I suppose. But when I'm following the T4T pattern of evangelism and discipleship I pray so much more. I do this because obedience to Christ requires one to walk in the Spirit of Christ, continually drawing on his power to bring about fruitfulness."

**2. The power of a changed life.** If you ask a new believer to explain the gospel to a lost skeptic, he or she may pause. But ask that same new believer to share what happened in their own life: their life before Jesus, how they met Jesus, and their life since Jesus, and they have a greater confidence. Who can argue with the story of what happened in my life? It is, after all, *my* story.

When T4T practitioners share their faith they are not initially sharing the gospel, but rather their testimony, i.e. the results of the gospel. These T4T practitioners know that lost people are blinded and deafened to the good news of what Christ has done for them. They do, however, like to hear about what happened to you. Initial sharing in T4T is a testimony of a changed life — your life. If it sparks an interest, the T4T practitioner then shares the gospel message — the reason for my changed life — in Lesson 1: Assurance of Salvation.

**3. The power of *oikos*** - A key 'hidden' reason why T4T has worked so remarkably in so many diverse cultures is that it rapidly moves beyond the first generation trainer into communities where lost persons are hearing from persons within their own culture While it is true that God desires everyone to know the good news of Jesus Christ – as Ying says: "All, not some" – new trainees can use some guidance in where to begin. For many of them, the thought of having to tell a hostile family member could inhibit them from sharing at all.

The first name list that a new trainee/disciple makes includes everyone in their *oikos*, the biblical term for family or network of close relationships that needs to know Jesus. There is a power in beginning with one's *oikos*. Your *oikos* speaks your language, shares your worldview, and has seen the change in your life. You know your *oikos* and your *oikos* knows you.

Even with this *oikos* name list, the new trainee might hesitate to share his or her own story of life change that Jesus has produced. Directing the trainee to pray and ask the Holy Spirit to show him or her the first five names to engage does several important things. It relocates the direction for sharing from the trainer to the Holy Spirit. Teaching the new trainee that we are truly working for God and not for any individual is key to transferring the movement to divine direction and momentum. Having the trainee prayerfully select which five persons he or she will share with first also increases the likelihood that those individuals will be most likely to say yes to the offer of the gospel. Once the trainee has one or two *oikos* members who have also embraced the gospel, it becomes easier to win the whole *oikos* and multiply churches among them.

**4. Doers of the Word.** If you haven't noticed, Ying and Grace are redefining the conventional understanding of discipleship from teaching to training. Teaching transmits knowledge; training changes behavior. In this way, the Kais are bringing us back to a New Testament understanding of true disciples as "doers of the Word" and not "hearers only." So long as Christians perceive of discipleship as knowledge or simply doctrine, they fall short of the life-changing, world-changing power of true discipleship. T4T develops a cadre of trained and training doers of the Word who obediently pursue Christ's commands.

**5. The 80/20 principle.** T4T is built on doers of the Word who hear and obey the Word of God. The sad reality is that most trainees will not prove to be doers of the Word. We can become frustrated with this reality, or we can acknowledge it and move on. The Kais, and most subsequent T4T trainers, have learned that as many as 80 percent of those we train will either not do what they've been trained to do, or fail to be fruitful themselves. The solution is not to quit, but to train 80 percent more disciples! It is not unusual for those who are initially not doers of the Word to later become fruitful doers of God's Word. So we must never give up on anyone, but we should invest our time in those who are do-ers of the Word. This sets a fruitful example for others to follow.

**6. Persons of peace.** Jesus promised that the Holy Spirit would be at work in the world convicting it of "guilt in regard to sin, judgment, and righteousness" (John 16:8). This means we can be assured that in every community with whom we share the gospel, there will be men and women who are already under the Holy Spirit's conviction. Jesus described these ripe fruit as persons of peace (Luke 10). It is a great blessing for the new trainee to go into the world, beginning with his or her own oikos, and know that there are persons in every community that the Holy Spirit has already prepared to respond positively to the gospel message that we bring.

**7. The power of accountability.** The world is filled with good evangelism and discipleship training. But too often, after the teacher leaves, the would-be disciples fail to implement what they have been taught. T4T uses Jesus's own model in Luke 10 to bring accountability to training. Just as Jesus called his disciples back to report to him what they had experienced when he sent them out two-by-two across the Galilee, so too we gather together those we train on a weekly or bi-weekly basis to report on what has happened. Not only does this group accountability increase effectiveness, it also provides a learning environment for these new disciples to learn from one another how to become more effective fishers of men and women.

**8. Super spreaders.** Explosive movements come when indi-vidual disciples are not only faithful in their witness, but prove to be God-anointed super spreaders of the gospel. Jesus hinted at this eventuality when he related the story of the four soils in Matthew 13:3-9. While a trainer may use the same training with each dis-ciple, for a variety of reasons some of them will not be fruitful. But faithful and persistent training will raise up some disciples who are extraordinarily gifted in producing fruit. Every movement gives evidence of a number of these highly fruitful individuals, these super spreaders. Movements are built on super spreaders.

**9. The T4T ethos.** Perhaps you've already grasped the spirit of T4T. The spirit goes beyond the mechanical activities involved in the training itself. Ying and Grace continually reinforce this spirit or ethos of T4T. The T4T ethos begins with believing we are doing the will of the Father, thus it involves prayerfulness, thankfulness, joy, a passion to share, a willingness to suffer, a humility that seeks the welfare of others above our own. T4T practitioners have a "can do" attitude. Ying and Grace use many means to encourage this ethos. If you miss it, you will reduce T4T to a mechanical exercise and soon lose your heart for what God desires.

**10. Small groups or churches.** When T4T movements produce hundreds and even thousands of small groups, observers have questioned whether or not these gatherings are churches or not. Christians have spent two thousand years debating the definition of church. The result is more than 40,000 denominations in our world today. Ying and Grace are strong believers in the importance of church and have dedicated the fourth of their seven foundational lessons to "The Church Gathering."

When Jesus commanded his followers to "make disciples of all nations" he knew that salvation and discipleship would result in churches. In T4T movements some of the small groups that emerge will grow into large traditional churches. Others, as a result of persecution or simply the constraints of their meeting places, will remain small and informal home groups, but churches nonetheless.

**11. Thanking God for all that comes.** When a T4T trainer or trainee sets out to obey Christ's Great Commission, Satan takes note. Satan is not infinite and must choose his battles well. So he focuses on those whom God would use to wrench souls away from the kingdom of darkness and bring them into the Kingdom of light. Ying and Grace have experienced numerous assaults from the Evil One as they have pursued God's vision for a lost world. You should expect nothing less. Ying has taught me (and Grace has taught him!) that the best defense we have for this spiritual battle is to thank God for everything that comes our way.

God's Word assures us that "all things work together for good to them that love God, to them who are the called according to his purpose" (Romans 8:28). Though we may not always see how God will turn the evil that we encounter into good, we can prayerfully thank God just the same, in faith believing that God will use it for good. As Ying has said, "If there is something we cannot thank God for, Satan will use it to drive us out of the ministry. So we must thank God as an expression of our belief that God will turn it to good purposes."

Now that we've explored the Hidden Wisdom of T4T, let's look at real-life examples of how T4T is expanding the Kingdom of God around the world.

# 10

# T4T Testimonies

Just as the Bible teaches that faith comes by hearing, so too does our faith in the power of Jesus's plan for pursuing a Church Planting Movement increase when we hear the testimonies of others who have gone before us. Here are some personal stories of T4T practitioners who have used this T4T plan and seen the Kingdom of God advance.

## MULTI-GENERATIONS IN UGANDA

The guards have started a new fellowship and they are having another baptism next Tuesday of about 25 or 30. We are starting some new T4T trainings among Muslims, and we are doing training with our team this weekend. Also, we are organizing our first Mid-Level Trainers Retreat. The Father continues to be at work and we are rejoicing in him; we have had about 35 new family members baptized in the last month.

Since December, we have had 108 baptisms, and started five or six new fellowships – all started by and run by Ugandans, producing multi-generational churches. We have two other churches starting this week, and 11 potential spots within the next month, and multiple trainings are ongoing so the potential is unlimited.

We now have a total of 13 groups, and many of the people are beginning to catch the vision. One of our groups is a third-generation group! So, now that we are using T4T, I think we are really going to see things take off. I believe that we could really see an explosion of groups over the next few months, which is our hearts' desire!

— A missionary in Uganda

## RUNNING RAPID IN INDIA

Last week our team and their disciples shared the gospel with 2,422 people, and 161 of them professed faith in Christ. We are leading over 200 training groups now. The numbers of people reached, saved, and in-training increases almost every week. Our local team is on track to reach 100,000 people in 2013, and to be leading 1000 training groups. So, Satan surely wants to attack us. That's why we desperately need your prayers.

As the Apostle Paul requested in 2 Thessalonians 3:1-2 "Finally, brethren, pray for us that the Word of the Lord will run rapidly and be glorified, just as it did also with you; and that we will be rescued from perverse and evil men..." This is also my request to you. Please pray for us, our team, the hundreds of new believers, and the thousands that will hear the gospel every week.

Suresh trained his disciple from Tamil Nadu to preach from creation to Christ by going with him to do it publicly. "Role play is good, but live-action training is better." He's storying in Tamil in Madrassi Colony.

Mohand cast vision to one of his 20 T4T trainees, explaining the map of the UUPGs – the unreached, unengaged people groups of South Asia, and teaching them how we can erase those red UUPG dots by multiplying workers and trainers. Preema came to the Lord a few months ago. She recently led four friends to Christ and baptized them!

Sara whom Suresh has been training since September now has 12 first-generation Training for Trainers groups and eight second-generation groups. In one group of 12 girls, seven have started their own groups.

Bharat is 15 years old. Just before Christmas Santosh led him to Christ. Bharat has started three T4T groups and Hasan his disciple, has started one too. But now Bharat's deranged father is forcing him to move back to a very backward and unreached area. So Santosh is pouring the Word into him this week, before he goes. We hope that by God's powerful grace he can start a church over there. Santosh will try to coach him. Please pray for Bharat.

Krishna, a new team member from Orissa, preached the gospel to 265 people in his first week and launched his first training group. Third-generation groups are starting to open. I expect that before summer we will be reaching 5,000 per week.

— Email from a missionary in India

## ECUADOR AND BEYOND

We moved to Cuenca, Ecuador in the Spring of 2009. We were sent out from our home church, WoodsEdge Community Church, in Spring, Texas with the goal of launching a church planting movement. We had a vision to see a CPM multiply throughout Ecuador and beyond, but lacked a simple strategy and practical tools. We struggled to see anything more than small gatherings of individuals in homes, without any multiplication.

Following an invitation to a T4T training conference in Wheaton, IL, in 2011, we were first introduced to the principles of T4T, and saw the biblical basis, its simplicity, and how it was working all over the world. In March of 2014, Ying Kai and Grace graciously agreed to come to Cuenca, Ecuador, and hold a T4T training conference for approximately 300 pastors and leaders from all over Ecuador.

One of the pastors, Mario Chuiza from Cuenca, asked Ying Kai, "If you could say just one thing to me, what would that be?"

Ying looked at him and said "Just do it!"

In the next 9 months, Mario's church of less than 50 people led more than 300 people to Christ, starting churches as far away as an hour and a half from Cuenca. The majority of the other pastors that attended were not receptive to the T4T training because of tradition and the paradigm shift it required in their ministry. But one pastor, who was unable to attend the conference because he was ill, called us and asked us to come replicate the training at his church in Quito. This started a chain reaction of word-of-mouth invitations to train all over Ecuador, Argentina and Uruguay.

In the two years that followed the implementation of T4T, 192 churches have been planted and there are now three streams of third-generation churches. Disciples are multiplying in the southern Andes Mountains, the Ecuadorian coast, and along the main north-south road that borders the Amazon jungle region.

One example of how well the T4T process is working in Latin America is in the city of Recreo, Ecuador. Pastor Giovanni Bohorques trained an initial group of 16 disciples in the T4T process. They began working in a very poor area on April 9 of 2016. In the first week, they led 71 people to Christ and began disciple making in 23 houses of peace with 5 to 9 people in each home. By Dec 31 of 2016, they had led 159 people to Christ, baptized 91, and had reached the third generation of disciples in two of their target areas. They have also planted churches along the northern coast of Ecuador by responding to the needs resulting from the series of severe earthquakes of 2016 with humanitarian efforts, and then abundantly sharing the gospel and discipling those who responded.

What made the difference for us? It was following the Bible-based T4T principles that includes prayer, sharing the gospel as soon as possible in any relationship in order to find God-prepared people, casting vision, using simple reproducing tools to disciple those new believers, and then equipping them to join in God's mission to reconcile the world.

Word of what is happening in Ecuador is spreading to other Latin American countries, and T4T training was requested by pastors and leaders in Argentina, Uruguay, and Peru. We now have a team of Ecuadorian pastors and leaders, from several different denominations, rising up to take responsibility together to see no place left in Ecuador (Romans 15:23).

Before T4T, even after more than 100 years of missionary work in Ecuador, the percentage of true followers of Jesus in the population as a whole was decreasing. T4T is a means to change that statistic, and the vision is now spreading throughout the nation of Ecuador...and beyond.

— Bob and Mary Burton, Ecuador

## HONDURAS

After being led by the Holy Spirit into learning about church-planting movements, we decided to invite Brother Ying and his wife Grace to come to Honduras and train pastors and church leaders in how to "make disciples that make disciples."

Ying and Grace came to Honduras in September 2015 and trained close to 400 people in three different cities: La Ceiba, San Pedro Sula and Tegucigalpa. We were powerfully impressed by his character and godly testimony of a life in close relationship with our Father. He was a great example both in method and attitude on how to teach the Word of God. His work as a team with Grace his wife was a delight to witness. They are humble servants who are helping the church to yield fruits that have not been seen since the times of the first church. T4T was an eye opener and soul changing experience. It changed the way we are making disciples.

Since his teachings we have adopted T4T as our disciple-making tool and have trained all the members of our local church how to train others to become disciples of Christ.

We have also been invited to other churches from our network and from other Christian affiliations to share T4T with them. Recently our network of CCI churches (300 churches on four continents) have come to the decision to embrace and train our church leaders in to the church-planting-movements paradigm.

We have also made the decision to join other Christian organizations around the globe to plant five million churches by 2020.

Thank you Ying and Grace. We hope you may come back to Honduras again.

— Allan Lorenzana, Senior Pastor of Centro Cristiano Internacional La Ceiba, Honduras

## SKYPING T4T IN EUROPE

After my time as an athlete I had the privilege to serve as sports chaplain at the Olympic Games in Sochi and in more than 20 world championship competitions around the world.

When Ying and Grace came to Europe in 2016, I was asked to serve as a translator for Ying. I later learned that God really wanted me to connect with Ying, and it was for much more than interpretation.

I was fascinated by the simplicity of T4T. I have always been looking for ways to help athletes and coaches best to grow in their faith when they are travelling so much to competitions and training camps. Professional athletes and coaches normally have no time on Sunday or even no church to go to where they can really grow spiritually in God's Word.

Two weeks after the conference, a Russian tennis coach visited us on his way to Spain. He stayed four days at our home with our family. We shared with him what great things God has done in our lives, and how my wife had faithfully prayed for him for 10 months. He told us his goal in life was to be happy, and he was. He called himself agnostic, believing only in a higher energy. Jesus didn't really make sense for him. However, on the fourth day of his visit, God's love hit him personally like fire. He confessed his sins and submitted his life to follow Jesus.

The next day I said to him let's start tomorrow morning with T4T on Skype together along with another soccer coach from Germany. That was our beginning with T4T on Skype. We met from 5:30-7:00 a.m.. During the first six months we met twice a week, sticking closely to the three-thirds pattern. And the results were simply amazing. Both of them were growing spiritually incredibly fast.

Soon after that the German soccer coach started his own T4T group, and the Russian tennis coach did so as well. Over the next weeks my wife and I started five other groups in the morning and one in the evening. Most of them were early in the morning from 5:30-7:00 a.m. before everyone goes about their daily life. We felt it was easier to organize in the morning. And Jesus is our role model as he got up early in the morning before dawn. So my wife and my alarm rings at 4:25 a.m. to start the day with prayer, God's Word, and to be prepared.

The more we grow in our identity as sons and daughters of our Father in heaven, the easier it has become to set goals. Our first two trainers even had the idea to start the day with worship together on Skype and now six times a week we have worship and prayer together on Skype from 5:30-6:00 a.m., and we are planning another meeting in the evening where all the other T4T family members can join.

People have said you can't do T4T in Europe like in China, but we just followed Ying's T4T training, made small adjustments and are seeing fruit that not only remains but multiplies. T4T became an amazing tool for us to train athletes and coaches to become trainers who train trainers, and after eight months, we are just getting started!

I see that if we really train trainers who train trainers out of our true identity as beloved sons and daughters of our good, good Father it is the greatest privilege. Motivated by his amazing love for us and others we all will be so much empowered beyond our wildest dreams if we obey his Great Commission and Great Commandment! Simply stated from the Father's heart: "God loves you. God saved you. Through you God wants to save all people who relate to you."

It has been such an honor for me to get to know Ying and Grace, their loving and encouraging hearts and faithful lives are role models in the service of our Lord Jesus Christ.

— Chaplain Jörg Wallach, Austria

## T4T REACHES AN IMAM

I'm not sure of the exact numbers, but we have had more than 80 decisions from folks in our people group since our meeting in November. One of those was an imam who came to Christ three days ago. We have six groups meeting that I feel pretty comfortable calling house churches. I expect to have one or two more by the end of the month.

I also expect to have four T4T training centers by the end of the month. We have had a dozen or so decisions from Muslims who are not in our people group. We have at least six who want to be baptized but I expect that number to greatly increase after new house churches get to the story of the Ethiopian official.

— A missionary in the Muslim world

## TIM'S LEGACY

I became a follower of Jesus as a teenager, and felt very strongly that God expected something of me.

One night, I was asking God to show me what to do, and suddenly there was a presence in the room of incredible power and peace, I felt I was in the presence of Jesus. He told me, "I have a mission for you, to reach people who will never darken the door of an ordinary church. I will send you to get the training you need to accomplish this mission and you will be my witness wherever I send you. I am about to open doors for you and I want you to walk through every door that opens. This is how you will know where to go, the door will open in front of you."

This changed the direction of my life; I applied to the university and then to the military academy at West Point. The doors opened for me, and I kept moving forward. While I was at West Point, I met Tim. Tim impressed me as he was one of the most Christlike persons I had met at that time. Everywhere he went people were moved to follow Jesus also because of his example. I admired Tim and watched him from a distance and attended small group with him for a couple of years. God was working on my character, and I still did not know how to help people the way Tim did.

Tim and I graduated in 2006 and both of us were posted to Fort Campbell, home of the 101st Airborne. Tim was an infantry officer and I was an engineer. At this time, I thought God had forgotten about me. I was newly married, and still didn't know how to make disciples. I was very frustrated and begged God to send me a mentor who could show me what to do. Tim suddenly showed up with his new wife having just graduated from Ranger School. I found him and asked him to help me, because I needed to learn more about Jesus. Tim was all excited, "Jeff, I have found the guys we have been looking for our whole lives, they can teach us how to make disciples of Jesus!"

Tim took me to a chapel where a group of sergeants and officers met during the week. I noticed immediately that there were a lot of young men who had recently started following Jesus and were learning about God from the Scriptures. I saw stuff happening that I had never seen before.

A few weeks later, we both deployed to combat operations in the north of Iraq. Around six months later, while eating in the mess hall, I learned that Tim had been killed a few hours earlier. I was shocked that God would take such a good man. I left the mess hall and went out into the Iraqi desert to pray. I asked God why he took Tim, and since Tim was gone, if he could use a guy like me to take Tim's place. I asked God to give me a double portion of the Spirit that was on Tim and promised him that when I got back to the U.S., I would find the men who Tim had introduced me to, and would dedicate my life to learning what Tim was trying to teach me.

After 15 months of operations, I returned to the U.S. and began to get training by a few men about how to train others. I stayed there for about 18 months and did another deployment and then moved to another post. I began to find that I loved to plant new ministries with my wife and co-laborers. I learned from Tim's wife that Tim had been praying Matthew 9:36-38 that I would become a laborer.

I began going into new places and planting new ministries. I watched people experience the ways that Ying Kai had been using T4T to reach large numbers of people and I began to experience it in the U.S. Army. Then one night God woke me up and told me to go back to my own part of the world to reach my own people. So I have come back to the Texas border with Mexico to begin training people who will reach all of South Texas and Northern Mexico until there is "no place left", not one man, woman, boy or girl who has not heard the good news about Jesus.

In 2010, our first son was born. I named him Timothy. I am filled with joy that each new believer, each new church, each family that is saved will be something that Tim can get credit for, because if I had not met Tim, I don't think I ever would have learned how to do this type of ministry for Jesus.

— Jeffrey Velázquez, Texas borderland

## T4T GLOBAL

Training for Trainers (T4T) is one of the most significant approaches to reaching lost humanity and enabling believers to become effective multipliers around the globe today.

I was Ying and Grace Kai's direct supervisor from 2000 - 2007 when they received training, began ministering, and facilitated amazing multiplication of new believers. My wife and I traveled with Ying and Grace, interviewed new believers and trainers, tabulated numbers, and verified miraculous stories from the original, remarkable, T4T movement.

The Kais attended training in October 2000 and began implementing Training for Trainers immediately. Within a few weeks, they facilitated old believers becoming effective evangelists and disciplers. Within a few months, new believers multiplied disciple makers.

Early on, I had the privilege of visiting the original training site, interviewing believers, and interviewing an old farmer who moved from being unfruitful to a fruitful multiplier of believers and churches. I regularly received verbal and written reports on the spread of the gospel in rural communities, suburban neighborhoods, inner city communities, factory dormitories, and expensive upper-crust compounds.

In 2007 I was privileged to be part of an assessment team that spent weeks interviewing, verifying, and tabulating numerical results and spiritual transformation. We verified new believers multiplying in house churches both nearby and far removed from the T4T ministry origination point.

Over the years I have received testimonies globally from Hindu, Islamic, nominal Christian, post Christian, Animist, Buddhist, and other communities where T4T has been effective.

## MY OBSERVATIONS OF T4T:

1. The secret is a godly man and woman, not the method. Leading a holy life.

2. Process, not content, of specific lessons.

3. Passion for lostness.

4. Focus on training every believer.

5. Prayer time spent on their knees for the lost and their trainees (2 Timothy 2:2).

6. Hospital chaplain accountability pattern he had practiced for years,

Ying and Grace have modeled, trained, and encouraged T4T in India, Thailand, South America, East Asia, Vietnam, Western Europe, the Middle East and elsewhere. The multiplying disciples in many nations are the result of godly men and women living holy lives, depending on God, and focusing on eliminating lostness as modeled for them by T4T trainers.

To God be the glory. Thank him for revealing this process to humble believers who developed it in East Asia and spread it globally.

May many catch his spirit, his passion for eliminating lostness, discipline to forgo frivolous activities, and fruitless ministries.

— Bill Smith, International Mission Board (SBC) Trainer

# PART TWO

*Stabilizing and Extending*

# 11

## Building a Healthy Movement

T4T is a great tool for giving new disciples, as well as older believers, clear direction for sharing their faith, discipling new believers, and training those new believers to do the same. As the movement grows, it becomes important for us to stabilize and extend the movement so that it does not pass away or lose its momentum.

### LONG-TERM SUSTAINABILITY
The key to long-term sustainability and T4T success is largely correlated with the training method. To achieve long-term sustainability, we must teach according to the Bible – while filled with the Spirit "to equip his people for works of service, so that the body of Christ may be built up" (Ephesians 4:12).

When someone is just starting with T4T, he may think it is enough to create a name list, share their testimony, and teach the seven lessons. It is incorrect to approach T4T with this type of mindset. T4T starts as a simple training method to allow every believer to share his or her testimony. Most believers in existing churches are able to immediately get started with T4T.

If you consider the number of opportunities to serve inside a 200-300 member church, there might be positions such as pastors, deacons, ministers, elders, Sunday school teachers, choir members, staff members, etc... for a total of around 40 to 50 positions. The remaining majority of the church members might think to themselves that there are no open positions to serve. As such, some of them only attend Sunday service (Sunday School or Sunday worship). Others, which would be considered great members, would either invite to church the people they know or share the gospel then. However, once they bring non-members to church, they might simply leave them in the hands of the church.

The T4T method is to train every believer to immediately evangelize and for them to personally train those they lead to Christ. In this way, they become disciples of Jesus. Following the teachings of Jesus, we bring each person before Christ and personally train them. In the same way, we lead them to use their training to train others. In this way, the teachings will be passed down from generation to generation. This method, which develops every new believer into a disciple who immediately starts to evangelize and train others will also cultivate their own spiritual growth.

T4T employs a simple method of teaching a new lesson so that those learning can fully comprehend and immediately utilize a repeated practice to gain full confidence in teaching the lesson. Those that are trained can then use this same approach the next day or the next week to train their own small group so that their small group will fully understand the lesson and teach the next generation. This method is simple, realistic, and practically reproducible.

As small group members (with each member who is also a trainer) train from generation to generation, you will often find that it is followed by additional needs and requests that go beyond the initial seven lessons. These needs and requests are based on the desire for trainers and their small groups to develop stable generational growth. They might include the need to nurture the trainers or the request for more Bible knowledge, pastoral care skills, a fruitful spiritual life, more spiritual gifts, etc.

Within each T4T outreach to a community, district, factory, university, or geographical area, you will find a need for mutual support, encouragement, communication, and partnership. This need arises as each trainer does his or her part within the body of Christ. During this time, the trainer should choose his group of close co-workers that will support each small group trainer working in the area. The trainer should also start his Mid-Level Training Retreat.

> **Equipping of the saints for the work of ministry,**
> **for the edifying of the body of Christ.**
> **(Ephesians 4:11-12; Romans 12:5-6)**

As the T4T movement reaches a point where there are many trainers and the area of influence expands even farther, local trainers can coordinate their efforts together and form an umbrella church network. While each church within the network, no matter how large or small, can be a church in its own rite with each member a part of the body of Christ (see Appendix Lesson 4), creating an umbrella network can allow for the sharing of resources and expansion of ministry and evangelism.

Trainers who lead Mid-Level Trainings need to prayerfully evaluate the different trainers in their group based on their specific spiritual gifts. They can then decide which workers would complement each other in this area and can serve all other trainers in the area.

## MID-LEVEL TRAINING

Mid-Level Training takes place some months after T4T training has been launched and a few generations of training groups have been formed. Mid-Level Training will serve to stabilize and extend the T4T movement as it grows into multiple levels of new disciples and trainers. As the movement grows you will identify men and women who share your heart and vision for the growing movement. We call these men and women "Big Trainers." Big Trainers are not higher in status or rank than any other trainer; we are all trainers – disciples of Jesus Christ – but Big Trainers are those individuals who are able to lead other trainers through Mid-Level Training to expand the work and strengthen it along the way.

The purpose and objective of Mid-Level Training is to prepare vessels for God's work in the spirit and power of Elijah. Elijah was a powerful servant of God through whom God was able to impact all those around him. Likewise John the Baptist, who prepared the people for the coming of the Lord, worked in the power and spirit of Elijah.

The Bible says: "And he will go before him in the spirit and power of Elijah, to turn the hearts of the fathers to the children, and the disobedient to the wisdom of the just, to make ready for the Lord a people prepared" (Luke 1:17).

God desires men and women who will serve him with the same spirit and power. How do we prepare a vessel for God's work in the spirit and power of Elijah?

After a period of time, many T4T trainers may have formed two or three groups. With multiplication of groups, there may even be third and fourth generations. It is typically at this point that many trainers begin to face challenges. Some of the challenges we often see include:

- Poor shepherding skills
- Problems with communication
- Inadequate life skills
- Lack of Bible knowledge
- Fatigue in the body, mind, and spirit
- Personal relationship problems with God, family, friends, and Christian co-workers

Therefore, we must support, sustain, counsel, help, and encourage them. If not, the small groups may experience problems, possibly to the point of disbanding. At this time, it is imperative that we select the most effective trainers, who are willing to accept training, for a Mid-Level Training Retreat that will span several days. Through this training, they will be strengthened to move forward and produce long-term results.

## SERVANTS OF THE LORD

We must recognize that T4T trainers are disciples of Jesus and servants of the Lord. Our desire is for every trainer to become a good and faithful servant of the Lord (Matthew 25:21; Luke 19:17) who is filled with the knowledge of the Lord and his word (2 Timothy 2:15).

There are three required characteristics of a servant of our Lord Jesus. Each characteristic is vital and none must be missing. As we train a good trainer, we must adhere to the commitment that they become a steadfast and loyal disciple who is filled with faith, goodness, and knowledge. Some disciples are very loyal and full of goodness, but lack wisdom and knowledge. Some are very smart, but not faithful nor good. Still others have been faithful and wise, and full of knowledge, but do not strive after purity and goodness. It is imperative that we, as servants of the Lord, must not be missing any of these three characteristics. As we train a good trainer, we must adhere to the belief that they become a steadfast and loyal disciple who is filled with faith, goodness, and knowledge.

Many people follow Jesus in a moment of enthusiasm. They will evangelize and even start training people. But after a period of time, there is no novelty in it any more and they lose interest. This is because they have not built a true intimate relationship with Jesus. They believed and even shared with others, but their heart's desire to serve the Lord was not strong. They had shallow and unstable roots, without the Holy Spirit's guidance and ability, so after a while their faith grew cold.

We cannot serve the Lord for amusement or as a hobby. Our willingness to serve should have its foundation in the desire to cooperate with the Holy Spirit. As we train a successful trainer, we must cultivate in them specific aspirations – a heart concentrated on following the Lord, a focused faith, experience walking alongside God, and a love for the souls of the lost. They must also have a heart for pastoral care and a deep and rich biblical knowledge. We need to ensure they link their lives with the life of the Lord Jesus. Only in this way will they truly serve God long term (1 Peter 1:13; 1 Timothy 4:13-16; 2 Timothy 4:2).

The trainer should also be able to cooperate with other trainers. They should build mutual trust, encouragement, exhortation, and support for one another (Romans 12:4-5; 1 Corinthians 12:26-27). This is why the T4T Mid-Level Training Retreat is so important. This can be considered one of the engines that drives the success of T4T. Just as important are the Big Trainers who are responsible for the trainings. They must ensure their guidance allows those who attend to truly receive help and encouragement (see Chapter 17 on Big Trainers).

As the movement grows, movement leaders will need partners who exhibit the skills and gifts that are needed to sustain and expand the movement. Trainers will need to watch for and cultivate co-workers who are able to contribute to the growth of the movement.

## DEVELOPING CO-WORKERS

There are important roles that must be addressed if the movement is to grow strong and healthy. As you train your trainers, look for co-workers who can fill these vital roles in the movement.

- **Prayer**. Prayer is an important job. Small group trainers may deal with issues regarding faith, family, work, school, etc. All of these issues require the person who prays to lift up and turn the issue over to God, praise him, and look to the Lord for guidance and help. Along the way, you will find that some have the spiritual gift for encouraging others and praying for them.

- **Pastoral care**. Many people can evangelize and establish training small groups. However, they may run into problems in pastoral care. Pastoral care, love, interpersonal relationships, Bible knowledge, and faith are all connected. As such, we need to pray for God to raise up partners who have all these spiritual gifts to help other co-workers.

- **Counseling**. This co-worker is able to comfort, encourage, help resolve issues, teach others to put down their burdens, and help lift one another up. It will require much prayer as we search for this important co-worker. As the movement grows, watch for those who, with proper training, can become good counselors.

- **Missions.** These co-workers have a visionary ambition to reach those far away. Their desire to spread the gospel does not stop at the local area but extends to far-off lands. In our current society, many people move to other cities or countries due to work, family, school, etc. These are opportunities for us to encourage them to become a missionary ambassador. These co-workers are the ones who have foresight and vision for the Kingdom of God.

- **Teaching.** There needs to be growth in both one's Christian life and the desire to increase their knowledge of God. Some people have the spiritual gift for teaching. Utilizing their spiritual knowledge and discernment, they can use simple methods to teach other trainers. Once those trainers have a better understanding of the truth, they will be able to better train others (Acts 18:24-28).

- **Visiting.** Among all the trainers, there will be those that experience setbacks, failures, or difficulties. We do not want to lose those who are struggling. During those times they need a co-worker who has the time and this spiritual gift to encourage and exhort them. These co-workers can pray with them to support them.

As your movement grows, each of these co-workers will become important partners in the development and maturation of this Kingdom work. No one can grow a health movement alone; it requires many members of the body of Christ working together. How do you find and train these co-workers? That's where the Mid-Level Training Retreat can help.

# 12

# The Mid-Level Retreat

When God begins to use the disciple of Jesus to produce fruit for his Kingdom, Satan takes notice. As they face Satan's attacks, T4T trainers may become tired, discouraged, or frustrated with the challenges of making and training many new disciples of Jesus. When this occurred in Jesus's ministry, he retreated with his disciples for quiet time of prayer, encouragement and training (Matthew 8:18, 17:1; John 3:22).

In the same way, you must plan periodic retreats with your trainers to pray with them, encourage them from God's Word, and train them for the challenges ahead. These Mid-Level Retreats are for the men and women who have proven to be fruitful trainers of others. About six to nine months into your training, schedule a retreat for those who have developed second, third or more generations of disciples for a Mid-Level Trainers Retreat.

As the movement grows into multiple levels of trainers, you will want to help your Big Trainers – men and women who share your heart and vision – to organize the trainers they are leading with their own Mid-Level Training for their trainers as well. In this way, the movement can continue to grow into multiple levels of trainers of trainers that will keep pace with the growing movement. The Mid-Level Training Retreat is divided into three parts.

## PART ONE: PASTORAL CARE AND COUNSELING

We begin this part of the retreat having each person introduce themselves in a small group. Then we ask them to discuss their family background, work status, evangelism experiences, and experiences leading their small group.

We know that these trainers have experienced great challenges in their ministry, so we schedule counselors to have personal time with each trainer during the retreat. This is a time for the trainer to discuss himself or herself, their family, work, living conditions, and their difficulties and blessings of leading their small groups. We ask our counselors to spend at least two hours with each trainer to pray with them, patiently guide them, and listen closely to their difficulties and problems. We encourage our counselors to listen more and talk less. It is important for the trainers to unload their burdens and know that they have been heard. The most important counseling is to pray for the trainers, encourage them, and bless them in every way possible.

During the time that counselors are meeting with some of the trainers, the other trainers can use this opportunity to read a predetermined book of the Bible. This book should be chosen with the intent to use it during the Bible teaching time in the second part of the retreat. Trainers can also utilize the time as a quiet time to think about their lives and their relationship with God. They will be able to learn how to independently be quiet before the Lord for contemplation, rest, relaxation, and laying down the burdens of their busy life to solely enjoy the blessing of being alone with God.

During group activity time, we lead the trainers to interactively experience help from one another. It's a good idea to separate the men and women into separate groups, so they will feel free to share openly about their struggles and needs.

We often use mutual trust exercises, such as leading one who is blindfolded. These exercises help to build harmony and camaraderie within the group. At the same time, within their small group of 10-15 trainers, we encourage them to develop their interpersonal relationships. One way to do this is by having everyone form a large circle, then based on each trainers knowledge of another trainer in the group, they will introduce the other trainer to the rest of the group.

The mid-level supervisor or Big Trainer encourages their trainers to speak the truth to one another in love and in the Lord. This is not a time to judge or attack one another, as the purpose is to allow each trainer to get to know himself or herself better. Within a small group of 10-15 people, each person will act as a mirror for one another. Revealing each person's view of another within the group is very important to encourage that person's personal growth.

If, in a group of 10 people, there are two or three people that see an issue with themselves or one of the other trainers that concerns them, but others in the group do not see that as an issue, then that person does not have to worry too much about it. On the other hand, if five or more in the group see some issue (interpersonal or spiritual), then that trainer should take note of the issue and prayerfully reflect on it.

If the majority of the trainers have the same view of one person, then that person should face it head on by asking the Lord to help him change. The supervisor, Big Trainer, should use wisdom and gentle words to guide each trainer in improving their shortcomings. Conversely, if the majority have a positive view of a trainer's specific attribute, then that trainer should appreciate, accept, and continue to develop that attribute. This is a very difficult and large building block of life that is not easy to work on. However, this is also a very important lesson to learn to be an effective servant of the Lord. After such an experience, the counseling and guidance given to each person will become a great support and encouragement to them.

## PART TWO: BIBLE KNOWLEDGE

There is no substitute for the Word of God in the life of the trainer. "For the Word of God is living and active. Sharper than any double-edged sword, it penetrates even to dividing soul and spirit, joints and marrow; it judges the thoughts and attitudes of the heart" (Hebrews 4:12).

The second part of the retreat typically lasts two to three days. During this time, we choose one book from the Bible to teach the trainers to satisfy their thirst for God's Word and give them more insight into the Word of God.

Following the T4T pattern, after the six basic lessons comes long-term Bible study (Lesson 7). In the weekly T4T meetings we select a few Bible verses then discuss them using the three S-O-S questions (What does the passage Say? What do we need to Obey? How do we Share this passage with others?). We use this same S-O-S method in our Mid-Level Trainers Retreat, but we apply it to an entire book of the Bible.

This simple and easily understood S-O-S method for studying the Bible gives disciples a deep and insightful understanding of God's Word over time. It should be noted that the downside to this method is that progress is slow, but we go slow to go deep and build strong. As trainer's desire for more in-depth Bible knowledge, their hearts will also yearn to be fulfilled with biblical knowledge. As such, we need to use this Mid-Level Retreat to teach them one whole book from the Bible. Typically, the first book chosen is one of Paul's letters such as Ephesians. Starting with the background and history of the letter, in a very detailed manner we teach them chapter-by-chapter, verse-by-verse. This teaching method will help them comprehend Bible knowledge over time for the whole book.

You can see the centrality of the Bible in T4T in the three ways the T4T trainer immerses his or her life in the Word of God.

1. Through daily devotions (see Lesson 3). We encourage each trainer to read three chapters from the Old Testament and one chapter from the New Testament each day. This enables the trainer to completely finish reading the Bible in one year. The purpose of this approach is to allow reading the entire Bible annually. Many believers often choose only portions of the Bible to read. As such, many times despite having been a believer for many years, they have not actually read the Bible all the way through.

2. Through the long-term S-O-S method. After completing the six basic T4T lessons, the seventh lesson teaches them how

to have a weekly inductive Bible study using the three simple S-O-S questions to obey God's will.

3. During the Mid-Level Training Retreat, in which we provide
a detailed Bible teaching time for one entire book of the
Bible.

These three points of Bible immersion help every believer/
trainer/disciple of the Lord get closer to God by building his and
her life around God's Word. In this way they will come to rely
on the Word of the Lord as an important building block for the
Christian life.

## PART THREE: REFLECT, RALLY, MOVE FORWARD

After a few days of small group activities, personal counseling,
quiet prayer, and cultivation of their Bible knowledge, the retreat
moves onto the third part. It is now time to rally and reorganize
before moving forward.

During this time each trainer will need to evaluate their own
small groups' conditions. Do they need to develop new name
lists needed for additional persons to evangelize and train?
Trainers need to develop an evangelism strategy for the next
6-12 months. Along the way, we encourage one another in small-
group interaction.

During the personal relationship training this time around,
each person should only offer supportive, encouraging, and exhorting words to one another with a positive attitude to expand
God's Kingdom. This will allow the small group to have a chance
to become a dynamic long-term training group with great interaction and mutual assistance.

The Big Trainer supervisor can now encourage each trainer to
schedule a bimonthly interactive meeting with those they train
in which they will share testimonies and encourage one another.
In this way the trainers will develop those they train into an extremely valuable elite group of disciples for God's Kingdom.

Within this third part, the mid-level supervisor, the Big Trainer, needs to have a counseling time for encouragement where he
prays for his trainers, commissioning them before sending them

out again. This time of rest and renewal allows them to recharge and go even further in the Lord's service.

The Mid-Level Retreat establishes a framework for trainers to have mutual support and encouragement. This will allow every trainer to feel that they are part of a community of believers living a life that is heaven on earth. As the Big Trainer guides the Mid-Level Retreat, he or she should pursue the following desired outcomes.

## MID-LEVEL RETREAT DESIRED OUTCOMES

### A. Pastoral Care: Directed to the Trainers

- Learning to listen – having the heart of a pastor/shepherd.
- Learning empathy – comforting people, exhibiting joy with those who are joyful and weeping with those who weep.
- Learning to fear the Lord – the fear of the Lord teaches you to love people.
- Learning to trust one another – we will not give up on anyone.

### B. Knowledge of the Bible: Directed to God

- Learning to know God – studying the Word of God.
- Learning to hear God – be moved by the Words of God so that you can hear him.
- Learning to obey God – respecting and obeying the will of God.
- Learning to live for God – always thinking of God and living for him.

### C. Interpersonal Development: Directed to One's Self

- Self-understanding – to grow and mature.
- Self-consideration – to love yourself.
- Training to have a pious attitude – to love God.
- Imitate Christ – to grow and improve.
- Leadership skills – to love others.

T4T Mid-Level Training Retreat helps to produce a Kingdom worker who loves God, loves others, and loves himself, so that they can make effective disciples of Christ.

## LOOKING AHEAD

Now that you have seen the role of the Mid-Level Training Retreat we can look more deeply into the nature of a T4T movement. What are the characteristics of an effective T4T trainer? What does the shepherd's heart look like? What are the most important lessons from the Bible that a T4T trainer must embrace? What does the prayer life of a T4T trainer develop? What is the role of theological training? How can T4T be used in existing churches to advance Christ's Kingdom?

# 13

# The Word and Prayer

As the T4T movement grows, reproducing disciples and churches, its firm foundation is built upon the Word of God and prayer.

Knowledge of the Bible is a life-long pursuit. For trainers a growing knowledge of the Bible is a priority. It helps to shape the DNA of the movement as it grows deeper and wider. Here are three dimensions to a growing knowledge of God's Word.

## FAMILIARITY WITH THE BIBLE

To gain familiarity with the Bible, it is okay to speed-read the Bible first. Then re-read it in-depth and aloud. As God brings special verses to your attention, you should memorize them so that the Lord's words are always in your heart.

It will be helpful for you to follow a daily Bible-study plan to ensure your progress in developing familiarity with God's Word. Then you can meditate on the Word of God day and night.

## USING GOD'S WORD

Developing a deep understanding of how to use God's Word requires meditating on God's Word, praying over it, and reading it repeatedly. Don't hesitate to examine and research reference books to better understand how others have viewed God's Word.

Give close attention to the key biblical themes. These themes address the core biblical revelations that answer the four major concerns that mankind has had since ancient times.

1. Where do we come from?

2. Why are we here?

3. How do we survive?

4. Where will we go in the future?

What is the connection between the Word of God and your livelihood, work, family, and yourself (Psalms 119:11)?

## IN-DEPTH BIBLE STUDY

Your knowledge of God's Word will deepen as you study the Bible chapter-by-chapter, verse-by-verse, sentence-by-sentence. Take time to learn the background of each book in the Bible, and receive the revelation that God has contained within it.

Ask the Holy Spirit to give you inspiration to understand the truth of God's Word. Jesus promised, "But when he, the Spirit of truth, comes, he will guide you into all truth." (John 16:13a). With the help of the Holy Spirit, you will be able to correctly handle the Word of truth (2 Timothy 2:15).

## THE POWER OF PRAYER

Bible knowledge apart from prayer is empty. Trainers must steep themselves in prayer in order to draw upon the power and will of the Holy Spirit as they grow into effective Kingdom workers. To reinforce the practice of prayer, we will review what we introduced in Lesson 2. This lesson is further expanded in the Mid-Level Retreat. Prayer is our primary connection to God and his will. Prayer is the source of all that we do for the Lord's Kingdom.

In short, we must pray...pray...and pray again!

Prayer is truly the most important link to God in our Christian life. If you do not prioritize prayer, your life will be depleted of energy. Without prayer, you will not be able to get close to God nor will you be able to hear his voice.

In the following paragraphs you can see what we teach our trainers about prayer.

## PRAY DAILY

It's important to schedule time each day to commune and pray with God, but you should also pray anywhere and at any time (Luke 6:12; Ephesians 6:18; Philippians 4:6). Remember, our Lord is with us at all times, so we should talk with him throughout the day and listen to him in each moment whether it be during a walk, a drive, or at work.

God is Spirit so we should commune with him in the Spirit and in truth (John 4:24) and enjoy our serenity within him.

## WHAT SHOULD WE PRAY ABOUT?

Pray for God's Kingdom to come as Jesus instructed in his model prayer – "thy Kingdom come." Pray for God's Kingdom to grow in your heart. Pray whenever you go out to begin your day. As you go, pray; pray when you ride in a car, drive a car, or walk. Pray for those around you. Pray for your city and country.

Pray for those persons on your name list that haven't yet been saved. Then pray for those you train and those they train. Pray for those who have received the training but have yet to evangelize or train others.

## PRAY IN JESUS'S NAME

Praying in the name of Jesus opens your heart to receive grace and mercy from Jesus. The Apostle Paul instructed us: "And whatever you do, whether in word or deed, do it all in the name of the Lord Jesus, giving thanks to God the Father through him" (Colossians 3:17). Remember that you are in a spiritual battle, so ask for Jesus's blood to protect you each day (Revelation 12:11). Ask God to send his angels and warriors to protect you.

Equip yourself with the armor of salvation daily, and so be safeguarded from the Evil One (Ephesians 6:11). In the midst of the battle, receive God's healing and comfort, and drive out evil from your life. Daily cleanse your body and soul (1 John 1:9). Continually examine yourself (Psalm 139:23) and so experience the Holy Spirit's transformation of your life and ministry.

## PRAYERS OF PRAISE AND VICTORY

Give thanks and praise for knowing Jesus, believing in him, and receiving forgiveness for your sins. In all things, and for all things, regardless of the time and place, give thanks to the Lord (Philippians 4:6). Praise the Lord with all your heart because we trust that God is Lord over everything (Romans 8:28). So give thanks to God for your environment, even when it seems unpleasant (Philippians 4:11-12). In this way, we can and should also pray for those who believe themselves to be our enemies (Matthew 5:44).

Pour out your heart when you speak with the Lord, giving prayers of praise and worship through psalms, hymns, and songs from the Spirit (Ephesians 5:19).

Praise God for the daily protection of being inside the Kingdom of the Son he loves. Give prayers of praise and thanks for allowing us to live in the camp of God's people and the city he loves. Pray for God's abundant preparations in your daily life.

## PRAYING WITH FAITH

Remember that prayer is not merely a formality or mantra; it should flow from the heart and be filled with faith and power. As you acknowledge the Lord and pursue intimate knowledge of him, you will be able to enjoy prayers of faith (Hosea 6:3).

Believe that you have received it. It will be yours as long as you ask according to God's will. As you trust the Lord, practice having faith in your prayers.

## THE JESUS PRAYER

Jesus gave us instructions on how to pray (Matthew 6:9-13). Fear the Lord, honor and respect him. Invite his Kingdom to come in your own life and ministry. In this way the Lord's will can work through you unobstructed. Now thank the Lord for what he has bestowed upon you. Love others and be loved by God and by others. Likewise, forgive others and allow them to forgive you. For as you forgive others, you will be forgiven, receiving Christ's grace and protection. As we live the prayer that Jesus modeled for us we will live in God's Kingdom, glory, and authority.

## THE FORM AND ATTITUDE OF PRAYER

What form and pattern should our prayers take? Pray at any time, place, and environment, but whenever possible, find a quiet place and pray earnestly. Pray aloud or within your heart.

## BIBLICAL MODELS FOR PRAYER

The Bible provides us with abundant models for prayer. Examine Enosh who called on the name of the Lord (Genesis 4:26). Consider Noah who gave thanks through sacrifice immediately after leaving the ark (Genesis 8:20).

Enoch, who walked with God daily (Genesis 5:22), can teach us how to enjoy being in the presence of the Lord. Father Abraham continually pleaded for sinners without giving up (Genesis 18:26-33). He always gave thanks to the Lord faithfully and is considered the father of faith (Hebrews 11:8-12). Abraham was also the first to tithe one tenth of his possessions (Genesis 14:20).

Abraham's son of promise, Isaac, meditated in the field (Genesis 24:63), and prayed for his barren wife (Genesis 25:21). God answered his prayers, and blessed them with twins. Isaac's son Jacob would not let go of God without a blessing (Genesis 32:26).

Remember, prayer is not about how long or short it is, or whether you are using poetic words. In every circumstance, you are communicating with God. Despite the worst of circumstances, the Bible tells us that Joseph relied on the Lord and the Lord caused him to prosper (Genesis 39:2).

When faced with overwhelming opposition, Moses raised his hands in prayer before the Lord to obtain victory (Exodus 17:11). Through prayer Joshua even stopped the sun and moon, stop the rotation of the earth. There was never a day like this before or after (Joshua 10:12-14).

Despite Samson's many failures, God gave Samson his strength once more to defeat the enemies of Israel (Judges 16:28-30).

When barren Hannah cried out to the Lord, God gave her a son. In return she gave her son Samuel to the Lord for all the days of his life (1 Samuel 1:10-28).

Who can forget the simple yet powerful prayer of Jabez who "...cried out ...'bless me and enlarge my territory'" (1 Chronicles 4:9-10).

The great king David sat humbly before the Lord and gave thanks to him (2 Samuel 7:18-21). David's son Solomon only asked God for wisdom and became famous throughout the world for his wisdom (1 Kings 3:9-22).

The prophet Elijah cried out loudly "answer me, Lord, answer me" and the Lord answered by sending fire upon his sacrifice (1 Kings 18:37-38). Likewise, Elijah prayed for neither dew nor rain on the land (1 Kings 17:1-2; James 5:17) and God granted his prayer. When he prayed again God made it rain (1 Kings 18:41-45; James 5:18).

Elijah's successor, Elisha prayed "Let me inherit a double portion of your spirit" (2 Kings 2:9-14) and God made him a great prophet.

As the prophet Daniel prayed, conflicts in the spiritual realm started (Daniel 10:12-21).

Esther prayed and fasted for God to save her people, and he did (Esther 4:15-16).

Nehemiah, who rebuilt the city walls of Jerusalem, was mentally praying to God even as he labored for God (Nehemiah 2:4-11).

Jesus prayed continually to his Father. Before choosing his twelve disciples, the Bible tells us Jesus prayed all night (Luke 6:12-13). As he completed our salvation on the cross, Jesus was communicating with his Father as he prayed, "Father, forgive them for they do not know what they are doing" (Luke 23:34).

The Apostles Peter and John prayed to heal the sick (Acts 3:1-7). Paul continued the pattern, praying to serve the Lord (Ephesians 6:18-20), and kneeled before the Father to pray for the church (Ephesians 3:14-16). He prayed for the thorn from his flesh to be removed but found God's grace to be sufficient (2 Corinthians 12:7-9).

The church in Jerusalem began with prayer (Acts 1:24). Then, as they organized, they prayerfully chose seven deacons (Acts 6:3-4). And when Peter was imprisoned, the church prayed earnestly for Peter's deliverance from prison (Acts 12:5-7), and God delivered him.

When T4T trainers walk prayerfully with the Lord, we are following in the footsteps of God's servants throughout the ages.

# 14

## Forward Together

As the T4T movement grows, a very important support column is the testimony and encouragement that occurs as the trainers meet together. Many people have a heart to work for the Lord and want to answer God's calling to serve the Lord. However, over time, if these individuals see little or no fruit, they may feel that they are not successful or effective. Eventually they may become discouraged and want to give up. Leaving their opportunity to serve due to disappointment is very unfortunate.

It is at this time, that we need to share with one another our testimonies, support, and encouragement. This is not just a time for sharing testimonies; rather it is the time to discuss the factors of success and failure, the experiences, and the lessons that we can learn through the counsel of one another. This will allow us to spur one another toward love and good deeds (Hebrews 10:24).

In our weekly meeting, as well as in our Mid-Level Retreat, we need to invite the trainers in the same community/area that have achieved great results and those that have not been able to achieve any results. Once one person has shared their testimony, experience, and situation, others can share their recommendations and encouragement.

This will allow everyone to share their own experience and approaches. This brainstorming of methods is very beneficial. Each person will be able to learn another's successful methods to

## At Shenzhen University

After attending our T4T training, a university student in Shenzhen started to prepare his lists. He decided to try and lead his professor to faith, but his professor objected, saying, "The universe is so big, how would I know if there is a God?"

The student then shared a story with the professor. When the Soviet Union sent the first astronauts into space, Khrushchev, the leader of the Soviet Union, spoke at a meeting of the United Nations, Khrushchev took off his shoe and beat it on the podium to get attention.

He said, "I have a very important announcement to make: our astronauts just went into space and they did not see God. This is proof that the universe does not have a God."

The next day, in The New York Times, Dr. Billy Graham shared this little story. "One day a worm came out of the Moscow subway station. He crawled around in a circle and said I will go back and tell the other earthworms, I have been in Moscow today and I do not see Khrushchev, so that is proof that there is no person called Khrushchev in Moscow."

The professor laughed at this joke. Moscow is such a big city, and he was a small earthworm. Just because you, the worm, did not see Khrushchev how are you able to declare there is no such person in Moscow?

Today, we all know that Khrushchev was the head of the Soviet Union. The whole world knows who he was, but in the story the worm was too small to see him. That does not give you the right to say Khrushchev doesn't exist.

Similarly, today's universe is so vast. How far did our astronauts reach? Can you imagine how big the solar system is? How small earth is within the solar system? How many solar systems and galaxies are in this universe? Just because there is no sighting of God in this solar system, how can we conclude there is no God?

After hearing this story, the professor laughed out loud and said, "This truly makes sense." He then said, "I am willing to believe in the existence of God, please tell me a more."

So the T4T trainer shared the gospel with him and led the professor to Jesus.

Praise God!

improve areas in which they were originally lacking or unsuccessful. Initially each person may feel that they are alone and need to figure out their own method, but now we have the thoughts from a collective group – this is a gift from God. This mutual support greatly increases each person's effectiveness.

## LOVE GOD, LOVE PEOPLE, LOVE YOURSELF – MAKE DISCIPLES

As trainers grow into effective Kingdom servants of the Lord, they must develop the personality of a shepherd, cultivate a caring heart, and grow in their interpersonal skills.

In 1 Timothy 3:1-13, the Apostle Paul describes the characteristics of those who would be shepherds (overseers and deacons) of the Lord's flock. Here are the qualities that we seek to develop in our trainers.

## BECOMING A SHEPHERD

Place great importance on prayer and being a shepherd (Acts 6:4). Becoming a shepherd is as important as being a member of God's family.

Feed regularly on God's Word and in prayer with God. Set regular time to spend with God (Matthew 24:45; Luke 12:42).

Base your pastoral care on the individual needs of your flock (1 Peter 5:2-23).

Care for each small group member's spiritual life so that they grow in maturity as they serve God's people (Ephesians 4:13).

Implement a pastoral-care plan for those you are leading.

Nurture "alpha" sheep. In each small group, there will always be an alpha. The alpha is the one who seems to automatically take responsibility to care for, help, and protect the group members.

## A CARING HEART

A shepherd's heart is an empathetic heart (Colossians 3:12-17; 3 John 3:2). So get to know every group member well and develop mutual trust within the group.

Take care for the spiritual, emotional, and physical health of the group members, giving attention to the needs of their family, work, and daily life concerns. At the same time, cultivate interaction, mutual assistance, support, and prayer between each member of the group.

Make the church the focal point of the group. Among the mountain people of Taiwan, where Grace and I ministered, whenever the people encounter problems or pick up a lost item, their first reaction is to head for the nearby church. The church is the center of their community. Your group should learn to do the same.

Help each member of your group to develop a testimony that they can share that fits within their life and livelihood.

## Two Doctors

One of our trainers led a doctor to the Lord. After making her decision for Christ, she really wanted her husband, who was also a doctor, to believe in Jesus. But he was not interested in listening or going to any Christian gatherings with her.

Her husband asked her, "What did I do to you that was not pleasing to you? Why must you believe in Jesus?" She replied, "You treated me very well, but this one thing is very important that you cannot give me: peace and joy in life. Only Jesus can do that."

She prayed every day for her husband, and even left a Bible and Jesus film on the living room table. When her husband came home from the hospital one day, he sat alone in the living room wondering just who is Jesus? So, he put on the Jesus film and after watching it, was moved. On his own, he knelt down to pray and accepted Jesus as his Savior.

When his wife returned home, he said to her, "Today, I was in the living room and saw you had left the video about of Jesus Christ and watched it.

I was deeply moved and have decided to accept Jesus as my Savior. I want Jesus to be the head of our home." Joyfully, the two of them, knelt down in prayer together. With thankful hearts, they decided to share Christ with both sides of their family.

Within a year, the two doctors led more than 30 friends and family members to faith in Christ.

We thank the Lord, the Father who saved them and through them saved all their friends and family.

## INTERPERSONAL RELATIONSHIP GROWTH

Pursue a mature Christian life, by learning to imitate Christ's model, building yourself up in your holy faith (Jude 1:20). Like Christ, we should be humble, loving, faithful, righteous, holy, and have mercy.

Exhibit the Holy Spirit's fruit in your life. The Holy Spirit expresses itself in the nine fruits of the Spirit (Galatians 5:22-23). Demonstrate a spirit of power, love, and self-discipline in the Lord (2 Timothy 1:7).

Learn to respect yourself and others, recognizing and controlling your emotions. Learn to serve others; be considerate, and accepting of everyone; learn to understand that everyone is created, loved, and blessed by God. Learn to grow within your environment – accept others view and suggestions.

Speak words of faith to live a victorious life as you learn to discern what can be shared with others and what should only be shared with God.

Learn to control every aspect of your life (body, mind, spirit, time, money, and character). Never say no way, or that's just the way I am!

# 15

## T4T in America

Since its beginnings in Asia in December 2000, T4T has spread to countries around the world, encountering diverse cultures and challenges. None of these challenges have been more substantial than those in the United States. On many occasions, North American church planters and missiologists have said, "It can't happen here!" Here are some testimonies of T4T practitioners who are seeing God's blessing of this Jesus method for Church Planting Movements in North America.

### VIRGINIA, KANSAS AND NEBRASKA

I was in Salem, Virginia looking forward to meeting with a young pastor who was considering doing T4T. We were to meet at a McDonald's. I got there a few minutes early and went to the counter to order. The lady at the counter who took my order looked a little sad, so I asked her this question: "How may I pray for you today?"

She said, "I think I am coming down with a cold and I have got a headache."

So I prayed for her work, her health, her relationships and that she would grow closer to God every day. When I opened my eyes, she was staring at me in wonder.

She exclaimed, "How did you do that?"

"Do what?" I replied.

"You made my headache go away and I feel great!"

I responded, "That wasn't me – that was the power of the Holy Spirit!"

Other customers came, so I took my food and enjoyed talking about T4T with my new friend. About 10 minutes later, the lady who was healed came to our table with another customer.

She said, "This lady is in terrible pain, would you pray for her too?"

We prayed, and this gave me the opportunity to encourage my new friend, and both the ladies, to start T4T groups with their friends and family.

Following my lead, one of my trainers, Lee, here in Omaha, started asking people the question, "How can I pray for you?"

One day he was having lunch with friends at a restaurant. He said to their server, "We will be praying for our meal soon, how may we pray for you?"

The server said, "Thank you! Please pray for my grandfather. He is old and in declining health."

Instead of leaving and going about his business, the server leaned in and joined the friends in prayer. Lee didn't think much about the incident until a couple of weeks later when he returned to the restaurant.

From a distance my trainer could see that the server was still working at the restaurant, but was working in a different section.

Lee thought, "I am rather shy and I don't want to bother the server – he probably doesn't remember me."

About that time the server came over to the trainer's table. He said, " Do you remember me?"

Lee called him by name and sheepishly admitted that he did and asked, "How is your grandfather doing?"

The man exclaimed, "He is doing great! He has been suffering from dementia for several years, but on the very day you prayed for him, his mind cleared and he has been better ever since. How did that happen?"

Lee explained the power of God's Holy Spirit and asked if the young man would like to study the Bible together. He said he would, and Lee started doing T4T training with the server and his family.

Let me share several different T4T stories from our area in Nebraska.

Doug Lee is based in North Platte, Nebraska. He started using a T4T strategy after many years of traditional church planting. He has started churches in Ogallala, North Platte, Alliance and Lexington. He works with Anglos, Native Americans, and Hispanics. He had 30 decisions for Christ in 2016.

Joel Wentworth is working the Sandhills of Nebraska and is working with two traditional churches, but recently started a house church with T4T principles. There are five families involved and they travel 20 miles to come. On Tuesday mornings he meets with six men at a bowling alley using T4T. Some of the men come 40 miles to get there. He is also working with another group of four close to his house at a local school.

Julie Arant is focused on international students in Omaha. She is excited to have over 100 students involved in church planting this year. They had 27 decisions for Christ in 2016. She is developing additional leadership and seeing generations within families coming to faith in Christ. Indians, Muslims, and Chinese are involved.

Dallas Powell and his wife Jen are working in Lincoln. He has a new Chinese church of 8-10 with three new leaders in Lincoln. He is also training a Karen (Burmese) church in Lincoln. He is working with my contacts in China with Northern Dong also. Since December 2016, he knows of three new churches started in China as a result of his training.

Lee Cordell is working with 12 church starts through Redeemer Church in Omaha. They had 14 decisions for Christ in 2016. Seven of those decisions were through Larry and Heather Derksen. They have third-generation growth. Larry and Heather were trained by Jan Wiehl. She continues to start new groups and is working with six groups right now.

Cheryl and I started a new T4T group this month. We have finished Lesson 2. So far we have had two decisions for Christ.

— John Mark Hanson, Nebraska

## SAN ANTONIO

In 2012 Jeff Sundell began to mentor us using T4T. My wife and I saw immediate results in evangelism, discipleship, and church planting.

I shared the biblical principles found in T4T with a young disciple I had been working with for a year. He was one of the same guys who had previously told me that what I had done with him was too complicated and he couldn't reproduce it. Using T4T he started his own group on Fort Sam Houston and went from 5 to 35 people in three weeks. He led several people to Christ in the coming weeks. On three separate occasions I witnessed four-week-old believers leading Bible studies. We had found a highly reproducible model of discipleship.

Since December 2012 we have trained 28 people to lead T4T groups and have seen three generations of groups and four generations of disciples. I should also mention here that we have also had several failed attempts at forming groups and churches. On the local level, when everything is put into perspective, God has done an incredible work here in San Antonio in the last year. But that is just the tip of the iceberg. In 2013, we have gone from two disciple-making groups to 17 (one considers itself a church). In addition, we have used the Internet to help start 111 groups around the country. We are now on-task to multiply to 2,020 disciple-making groups and churches by 2020.

Since that time the Lord Jesus has blessed our efforts on six continents with hundreds of new disciples and churches using T4T for his glory. We actually met Ying and Grace Kai at a training event, and were struck by their humility and love for people. We had the wonderful privilege to personally thank them for their huge contribution in our lives. Words cannot express our gratitude for these faithful saints who day in and day out train people to share the gospel and make disciples. Ying and Grace are an amazing couple. May the Lord Jesus Christ continue to multiply their efforts around the globe.

T4T works! But I need to bring some perspective into the story at this point. T4T is a method. It works because of the biblical principles it is founded on.

— Chuck and Deb Wood, San Antonio

## HAMTRAMCK, MICHIGAN

Over six years ago God gave me a dream in which I saw the word "Hamtramck" and two people's faces. I didn't think that "Hamtramck" was a word (it doesn't have enough vowels), and so shrugged it off, but a month later I found myself visiting Hamtramck, Michigan with my campus ministry from the University of Pittsburgh Johnstown in Pennsylvania. I met the two people in my dream, and a few months later I packed up my belongings and started ministry in Hamtramck.

Hamtramck is a two square mile area inside the city limits of Detroit. It is one of the most ethnically diverse areas in the United States. The majority of the people are Muslims, most of whom come from restricted nations and have not heard the gospel. There are currently over 15 mosques within the city, and the call to prayer sounds five times a day.

Around 2011 I read David Garrison's seminal work Church Planting Movements and was hooked. I was astonished by what God was doing, and instantly captured by an insatiable hunger to be a part of disciples making disciples and churches planting churches throughout the nation and the world. I no longer just wanted to lead someone to Christ. I wanted to see a movement of apostles, prophets, evangelists, pastors, and teachers raised out of lostness to reach their own communities.

Sometime after that, a co-laborer told me about a missionary named Jeff Sundell who had seen massive movements in Asia and was experimenting with T4T and church-planting movements here in the United States. I began watching Jeff Sundell's YouTube training videos over and over again. It took us a few months to realize that we were making drastic mistakes.

My co-laborer called for help from someone he knew during his time in the military, who he had heard was now seeing movements. Around late 2012 early 2013 we began meeting weekly with Chuck Wood over video conference. His mentorship not only helped me grow immensely in effectiveness in reaching the lost and making disciples, but also in my personal life and relationship with the Lord.

T4T gave me practical steps to obey the Great Commission and help others do that as well, regardless of situation, context, or resources.

Beyond any strategy or method, making disciples has taught me perseverance. You have to persevere. I am living in the answer to prayers I prayed years ago, but for years the work seemed discouraging. I saw numerous people make decisions for Christ and then fall away. I saw 53 groups start and disband before I stopped counting. I saw God do numerous miracles, supernaturally healing both Hindus and Muslims, but saw them still reject the gospel. I saw Muslims make decisions for Christ, only to turn away when they were persecuted or tempted. I remember knocking on doors to hand out Jesus films in the rain and thinking to myself, "I hate this." Many times it seemed like everything was failing.

God kept me going and kept me obeying him until I saw fruit. I cannot thank Chuck Wood enough. I used to meet with him every week, and I was so discouraged and frustrated. Every week he talked me off the ledge and encouraged me.

I had to learn to see beyond the difficulty. I was called. I was hooked. I was bitten by a vision that I couldn't walk away from even if I wanted to. I remember thinking, "What can I do? I can't think of anything that Jesus wants more than a harvest of disciples. I can't think of anything that glorifies God more than a movement that produces thousands of people who enter into a love relationship with Him. This is what I have to do." The vision is still so big in my heart.

I remember being at a T4T conference and crying myself to sleep in my hotel bed each night because I wasn't seeing fruit. At that conference, I met two people who wanted me to train them. Today they are the most fruitful people I've trained, multiplying over 15 church starts. God answers prayer.

God's work in Hamtramck has just begun. I'm standing on the shoulders of those who have gone before me and the teammates and co-laborers who support me. We currently have two churches and numerous discovery Bible studies with people from Yemen, Bangladesh, Eastern Europe, and more. Our small network has seen over 20 baptisms and seen leaders emerge who have gone on to practice T4T and disciple making in new cities and new nations. The very best is yet to come.

— Jonathan Ammon, Hamtramck, Michigan

## T4T IN THE ARMY

For years I participated in discipleship ministries that greatly assisted in grounding my faith in the Word of God, prayer, fellowship and serving others. However, like many I really struggled with witnessing and sharing the gospel. I was excited about sharpening with other Christians, but hesitated about sharing with those I suspected were hostile to the gospel. I had a great desire to see believers grow into maturity, but spreading the gospel to the un-evangelized was a struggle.

When my wife and I were exposed to T4T, it was like nothing I had ever quite seen before. It made simple what in my mind had become a mountain. Starting with prayer and the Great Commission from Jesus, my heart was fueled as I looked over my name lists and the Lord starting laying specific things on my heart to pray for them.

I quickly found myself in conversation with these men and remembering my prayers for them would share my testimony and the gospel. Within a few months I had started two groups in addition to meeting with a few individuals, and in the process I experienced a new level of participation in God's Kingdom I had never known before. I had always had the desire, but Holy Spirit moved through the teaching T4T gave me and changed my heart regarding how I saw others. Now he is using me to confidently lead others to understand who they are in Christ, and send them to their oikos!

When the Army sent me to Qatar and Afghanistan, I started two more groups. God was faithful and he put men in our path that loved Jesus and started changing the focus from traditional Bible studies to equipping. And God did! Soon men on the base from all four corners of the globe started to hear about Jesus in the chow hall, in hallways, and in every routine task in life. Many of the men in these groups have continued to be faithful, and since that time equipping work has gone on in Louisiana, North Carolina, New York, Afghanistan, Kenya, and the Philippines.

— Adam Patten, US Army

## A REPRODUCIBLE METHOD

Ying's development of Training for Trainers (T4T) has inspired me in so many areas, breaking the mold in which I found myself for many years of ministry. The practice of training new believers to immediately share their faith was something I had never considered. But I decided to put it into practice.

Jim came to me for advice about his struggling marriage. I asked him to tell me about his spiritual journey. When I realized that Jim had never embraced Jesus as his Lord and Savior, I shared the gospel with him using a very reproducible method. Jim believed! Three days later, I shared with his wife, using the same reproducible method, and she believed! I told them I would love to begin a Bible study with them in their home. They said that would be great, and said, "We can start tonight!"

Even though I had not officially trained him how to share the gospel, Jim had now seen the simple tool twice. So later that afternoon, I sent a text message to him and said that I'd like for him to share the gospel with his children when I came over that night. I assured him that I'd be there to help him if he got stuck. To my amazement, Jim agreed!

That evening, with very little input from me, I witnessed Jim reproduce the same gospel presentation I'd shared with him and his wife. AND HIS TWO OLDEST CHILDREN BELIEVED! I knew in that moment that Training for Trainers was not just "a China thing." It was God's gift to the global church to spark a movement of reproducing disciples.

— Peter Horn, Senior Pastor, Hill Country Bible Church,
Leander, Texas

## I'M READY!

In the fall of 2015 we, as a team, decided to go meet and care for our neighbors. We introduced ourselves simply by stating, "Hi my name is Garret and this is my friend Ronnie. We're out caring for the community today and we are wondering if there is anything you or your family need that we could pray and ask God to help you with."

We met one neighbor named John. After offering care through prayer to John, he laughed and said, "Yeah, you can pray for me. Last night I had a dream that I knew was from God. I woke up and knew God wanted me to change my life. Now you guys are here. So, yeah, you can pray for me."

After praying a short, simple prayer, we asked, "Would you mind if we came back another day at another time? We'd love to share a story with you!"

We agreed on a good time to return, thanked John for his time, and then left.

Upon returning a few days later, John gladly welcomed us into his home. Sitting in his home, with his family attentively listening, we proceeded to share a story about Jesus with him. After telling the Jesus story, we shared our own stories about how God had changed our lives. After hearing our stories, John decided that he wanted to walk with Jesus. We showed him the Great Commission and what it means to be a follower and a fisher of men. As we got to baptism, and explained its symbolism, John promptly took off his shoes. He walked outside and, while still wearing his blue jeans, stepped into his swimming pool. He exclaimed, "If that is what Jesus wants me to do, I'll do it right now! I'm ready."

We baptized John that day and all celebrated together. A few weeks later, John led his mom to Christ and baptized her. A few weeks after that, he baptized his brother. Then, just a few months ago, his dad was baptized. John has led many to Jesus in his own sphere of influence, as well as those in his community.

We've seen this reality to be true: all across our city there are people just like John. There are people who are hungry for something more, longing to know truth, and in need of a neighbor, or someone in their sphere of influence, to care enough about them to engage with them in a loving way. We are asking God to raise up an army from the Bride of Christ to go and care for those around them, who are far from God, so that our city may shine brightly with the glory of God in a way that ripples to the ends of the earth.

— Garret, No Place Left, Austin, Texas

## FROM NEW YORK TO AFRICA

Here is our testimony of what we have seen the Lord do since we started obeying Jesus through the T4T model.

While in New York we were originally in a small traditional church and saw very little growth. For the last six months we were there, we began to implement the T4T model and saw 54 persons come to faith and baptism. The shift from knowledge-based training to obedience-based training, and using the three-thirds process were instrumental in helping people hear from the Lord and become used to obeying Jesus's voice.

Then we implemented T4T in Washington D.C. for about a year. We saw 108 persons baptized and we saw 16 churches start. Additionally, we saw seven generations of disciples born within three weeks.

We then moved to West Africa as tent makers (lay missionaries with secular employment). We worked full time as diplomats in the US Embassy, but our main mission was as ambassadors of Jesus Christ. We very quickly formed a small church with several young uneducated guys. I was very direct and told them that I didn't have time to just teach them but that everything I taught them was meant to be taught to everyone else.

Once they caught the vision that multiplication was meant to continue forever, the movement took off in the Holy Spirit's hands. Through that small church of 10-15 guys we saw over 10,000 baptisms, 27 generations of churches in five African countries and approximately 1,200 churches. The best part is that most of the growth came during a five-month period when I was out of the continent. My absence freed the guys up to travel much more and plant more churches throughout the rural villages.

Our numbers are not exact, but a conservative estimate. Because most of the people in the network of churches had full-time jobs; they had a hard time keeping track of all the baptisms and new church plants. One of the third-generation churches was in a very dry location with no access to a body of water for baptism. They continued to lead people to Christ and we eventually bought a pool to be used by many of the new church plants. The first day the pool was installed they baptized over 500 people.

What we love most about T4T is that it presents the model of ministry Jesus used. It empowers everyone to fulfill the calling that Jesus gave us all. And, it allows the tent-builder missionaries to bear much fruit and so show ourselves to be his disciples (John 15:8). Our time in Africa and the fruit we saw is a complete testimony to the power of the Holy Spirit. We really only spent a lot of time with our first 10-person church. We prayed a lot; loved a lot; taught a lot; empowered a lot; and tracked numbers a lot. So, when we left Africa and saw over 10,000 baptized we could really give ALL the Glory to the Holy Spirit; only he could accomplish such a miracle.

We love you Ying and Grace. You guys have impacted our lives more than you know. We appreciate your teachings and trainings, but are most thankful for your love, prayers and your friendship. When I consider 1 Corinthians 11:1 and what I want to emulate from you, Ying, it's how well you love other people. I want to love people like you love people because you love people how Jesus loves people.

— JBM, pseudonymized for security purposes

## INDIANA AND BEYOND

I was mentored in movement principles for 10 years in Indianapolis, Indiana, and personally saw zero impact on lostness until 2011, when Steve Parlato introduced me to the simple, biblical, T4T process. The T4T three-thirds format provided the handles I needed to simply begin obeying Jesus's Great Commission "on Monday morning" and equip others to do the same. I was challenged by the God-sized vision and encouraged to trust the Heavenly Father's heart for the harvest.

We immediately began sharing the gospel with lost people and equipped believers to make disciples. Within a month, we saw multiple streams of fourth-generation new believers and discipleship groups among high school students, neighbors, families, pastors, and churches. We have since seen God multiply disciples, groups, and churches across North America, in East Asia, the Caribbean and Central America.

— Troy Cooper, Indiana and Florida

## ONWARD CHURCH

Onward Church was born out of a burden that the Lord had been placing on my heart for some time. I started my ministry as a pastor in 1990 in the usual way of "attractional" church. The traditional idea of "doing church" was to develop a program on Sundays that would draw those who were far from God to hear the gospel and connect with the Lord and his people. But after more than 20 years doing it this way, something seemed very ineffective to me with this approach.

I've said for a long time, "I'm way too old to play church!" I love Jesus and want people to come to know him. The way we had been doing the job of the Great Commission just didn't seem to be working as well as it should. As a friend has said, "We are losing our cities at supersonic speed." There had to be a different way of accomplishing the mission that Jesus commanded us to do.

About that time I was introduced to the story of Ying Kai. In 2001 Ying Kai had been assigned as a missionary to an unreached people group of 20 million people in a country in the Far East. But as he considered the overwhelming responsibility of trying to have an impact on 20 million people, he realized that if he kept doing what he had been doing he would never make a dent in reaching these unreached people. As he turned to the Lord in prayer and meditated on the Great Commission (Matthew 28:18-20), the Lord's instructions for pursuing his new assignment were there. The Great Commission instructs that we are to go, not invite them to come to us; that everyone is to be engaged in attempting to reach everyone, everywhere; and we are to make disciples, not just church members or converts.

With these new marching orders, Ying Kai began a movement that was responsible for seeing more than 1.7 million people baptized and more than 150,000 new churches started. This story was overwhelming to me.

For the 10 years prior to starting Onward, I had served in a church plant that was 10 years old and was among the top one percent most successful church plants in America. In its 10-year history (2001 to 2011) it had grown from zero to 1,500 in worship and baptized 1,000 people —covering the same 10 years as Ying Kai's work in the Far East...1000 compared to 1,700,000.

I came to the realization that in my years as a pastor I had encouraged, challenged, rebuked, motivated, inspired and even scolded Christians toward disciple-making, but I had never taught them how to make a disciple. As a matter of fact, it had never occurred to me that my first responsibility as a pastor in "equipping the saints for the work of ministry" (Ephesians 4:11-13) was to teach them how to make disciples who were able to make disciples (2 Timothy 2:2). I asked the Lord for forgiveness and determined to train everyone in disciple-making using the principles of T4T.

So this is our purpose and our mission: to teach how to make disciples...And not just to make disciples, but to make disciples who know how to make disciples. Ying Kai called these people "trainers." The idea is to train trainers who can train trainers. It is in the built-in multiplication process that we see the explosion of the work of God by sending many workers into his harvest (Matthew 9:37-38). Therefore we are training all of our people to be able to make disciples using the principles that Ying Kai developed in T4T. What can God do through us in the months and years ahead if we can learn to be effective in making disciples who can make disciples?

T4T contains brilliant concepts and processes that are often difficult to internalize. Many of the principles that Ying Kai has developed, while thoroughly biblical, are so foreign to the paradigm of American church, that pastors often have difficulty in understanding and applying them.

Using T4T over the next couple of years we were able to track more than six streams of sixth-generation believers that began with our training. We learned that letting go of ministry was very important. Trying to hold onto the people in a disciple-making movement creates a bottleneck that inhibits growth. That's why we "commissioned" all of our trainers (disciple-makers) to be baptizers.

As we divided the people in our new church plant (January 2012) into training groups we started with eight groups containing on the average 25 people per group. We met every other week as Ying suggests so that they would have time in their schedule to train others.

A number of people fell away as we trained them, but in the end 120 went all the way through the training and began sharing their faith, leading people to Christ and immediately leading them through the training they had received.

Our initial eight training groups ran from January through May. In June, we launched 20 new groups. By September we had "grown them down" to 12 groups. In other words many of the groups had disbanded or failed. We were disappointed with the results although determined to persevere—especially since Jesus didn't give us the mission of the Great Commission as "Plan A," and another mission as "Plan B" if the first mission was too challenging!

We developed our training materials around the three-thirds process—even including this format in our Sunday message outlines. We also learned that people in America seemed to want "big church" that met on Sunday mornings, and "small church" that met during the week in homes. This seemed to be not too unlike the early Jerusalem church, which "worshipped at the Temple, and met in homes."

Tracking the results of our training has been difficult. For me, it doesn't matter. We know we have well in excess of 300 groups today, which include over 3,000 people. Once we get out about four generations we have had little success in knowing what is happening. We have estimated that more than 1,000 have been baptized and yet I estimate that more than 80 percent of the people in our groups, and those who have been reached, don't know my name! But they know Jesus! And that's all that matters to me.

— Gary Stump, Founding Pastor, Onward Church

# PART THREE

## Maturing Movements

# 16

# T4T in Existing Churches

Pastors often ask me, "How can I use T4T in my church? If you were the pastor of my church, how would you do it?"

I have been a pastor too, so I understand their question. I think the most important thing is the need to lay down our old traditional pastor concepts. We need to completely return to Jesus's Great Commission and start to realize the strategy Jesus gave us to share the gospel and establish the Kingdom of God.

## START WITH THE PASTORAL STAFF

If your church has a pastoral staff, then you must first communicate with the elders and the deacons. Next, during your Sunday sermon, you should share Jesus's strategy for evangelism in order to have a united vision within your entire church. Helping everyone to have the same heart within the Lord is the first priority.

You will need to train every pastoral staff member including elders and deacons, so that they can start their own training groups.

These trainings will then need to expand to include every church member so that they will receive the same training. Remember to never have the thought of choosing who is or is not qualified. Every Christian is qualified to become a disciple of Jesus.

## TRAIN EVERY CHURCH MEMBER

Do not limit who to train – train every believer starting from the basics and share with them Jesus's Great Commission. Have each person write down their testimony that will be used for sharing. Each believer may have multiple testimonies, but it is important to limit the testimonies to two to three in which their lives were most affected. They should then pray, think, and write down their name list. This list should include names of those around them who are not yet believers as well as believers they can train. Once written down, they should pray for each person on their name list.

You must not limit who goes on your name list; rather, let the Holy Spirit choose who will become a person of peace. Training every member is our responsibility as a minister. The Holy Spirit designates whom the person of peace is – man sees what is outside, but the Holy Spirit sees what is inside. We must not give up on any church member, but continue to exhort, encourage, and teach them. You never know when a member will suddenly be moved by the Holy Spirit to have an increased passion for evangelism. So continue to pray as you work.

## CONTINUOUS DEVELOPMENT AND TRAINING

There are times a church needs to be transformed from a traditional mode to that of obeying Jesus's Great Commission – manifested by having every believer become a trainer then a disciple. Not everyone will accept this mode after a single T4T training. It is important to understand that within a church, there are senior members who are only use to performing routine tasks but not evangelizing.

There are also members who have the habit of only sending others or the pastor for evangelism. Over the years, there may even be those who merely listen but do not act. These members are capable of detailed discussions on sermons and may even check on which reference books the sermon used, but they do not act on the message of the sermon. There are also those who attend church regularly throughout the year but do not care for the truth. If you were to ask them whether they identify themselves as Christians, they will immediately respond "Yes" but they may never have the desire to live out a Christian life.

Even still are those who are very passionate in studying their Bible and serve in multiple roles within the church. However, if these are merely interests to them, their passion of serving will not last long. A church is made up of many different types of members. This is the typical pattern in today's churches that stems from thoughts and traditions that are passed down to us throughout the generations.

To have practical training sessions time and time again, we must perform them with patience, faith, and determination. From our experience, each training will only have around 15-20 percent of attendees who are willing and have the desire to apply the methods we teach. It is important to never give up on continuous training and encouragement. Eventually, the majority of the church members will come to understand and be willing to participate.

## DEVELOPMENT FOLLOW-UP
Once the majority of church members have started practical evangelism and small group training, you need to organize the trainers into groups, focusing on the trainers who have exceptional organizational skills to lead each of those groups. These leaders will need to establish a group of trainers (once every two to three months) to share testimonies, encouragement, and sharing meetings (refer back to Chapter 8: The T4T Process).

Following this process, we can use Mid-Level Retreats to effectively help, inspire, and lead small group trainers to learn from each other and motivate each other so their small groups can stabilize and continue to grow.

## SPIRITUAL GROWTH
The experience of leading people to the Lord, then training and cultivating new believers so that those new believers can also train and cultivate other new believers is a deeper level of life

experience. This level will help the Christian life grow in abundance. Our goal is to have every believer enjoy the Christian life – to feel what it is like to be a true disciple of God.

I have asked many church members if they believe in Jesus. They replied, "Of course I believe!" I would then ask, "Are you a Christian?" They would respond, "Of course I am!" If I then follow up with, "Have you obeyed the commands of Christ?" They begin to hesitate.

If I then ask, "Are you truly a disciple of Jesus?" they would either not answer, be unsure, or say something along the lines of "I dare not be." Why is this? Jesus surely instructed us to make them into his disciples. If we share the gospel but do not lead them to become disciples, then that means we did not do our duty and are insufficient as God's workers. The Lord's church should be comprised of disciples of the Lord. They should continuously fulfill the Lord's commandment until the whole world is filled with disciples of the Lord.

## ONGOING TRAINING

Theological training is an integral part of a growing T4T movement and something that we can draw from traditional churches and seminaries to provide. As the movement begins to change every follower into a disciple of the Lord, the disciples will begin to evangelize, train others, and have an increasing desire for more biblical knowledge. It will be necessary to equip them with theological education so that they have a more complete biblical knowledge, maintain a pure faith, good church management strategies, and a vision for the expansion of God's Kingdom.

What we build with is gold and silver and not hay or straw (1 Corinthians 3:11-13). Therefore we must train our disciples with the most holy faith and build the Lord's church on the rock.

We extend invitations to qualified pastors and seminary professors to equip our trainers. This is done in an effort to support each trainer in attending at least five basic theological courses.

How do we become a good servant and shepherd? How do we take care of our flock? How do we care for the growth of our church? This is the work of pastoral care and should never be neglected as the movement of new disciples takes place.

Apologetics, the defense of the faith, should also grow with the development of the movement. Each context has its own apologetic needs. Since the earliest years of the church, many pagan ideas and heresies have plagued the church. Satan often sandwiches false teachings between biblical truths. Such situations can confuse faithful believers. That is why correct doctrine and apologetics is very important! As the movement grows, trainers can learn from one another as well as from seminary-trained leaders how best to answer the questions that lost persons bring to the gospel conversation.

Not every trainer has the gift of teaching or training, but along the way, we will see individuals emerge who have a gift and calling for preaching the Word of God. For this reason, we need to teach them basic skills for sharing the Word of the Lord, so that they will be more confident as they serve the Lord and preach the good news.

Every servant of the Lord must obey the Great Commission to spread the gospel over the whole world. To become more effective in this pursuit, we need greater missional understanding. Well-equipped trainers will not only share the gospel in their own area, but also spread the gospel into places that have never heard the gospel. Good missiology training can equip disciples to extend the movement to the ends of the earth.

Since apostolic times, the church has been an organization that needs the election of deacons to manage the affairs of the church. As the movement grows, trainers need to have general church administrative training to compliment trainers to build healthy churches.

As new churches grow, some trainers will feel called into full-time service and desire to equip themselves further. We should help introduce them to pure-faith seminary teachings.

T4T never exists apart from the church. It exists to strengthen the church, expand its witness, and establish new and healthy churches among every people group, tribe, and tongue. In the same way, existing churches and theological seminaries can contribute to the deepening and strengthening of growing T4T movements.

In the next chapter we will examine how God raises up gifted trainers to take on the roles of deacons, elders, missionaries, pastoral care givers, and theological trainers. These important members of the growing movement are found in the emergence of Big Trainers.

# 17

## Big Trainers

From the very first meeting of T4T training, you should take note to find future loyal co-workers who are easy to collaborate with. These trainers will emerge as Big Trainers or Senior Trainers. It is important that we not be hasty in choosing these Big Trainers.

A Big Trainer is a co-laborer, not a position of authority or hierarchy in the movement. A Big Trainer is a partner, but not someone who is elevated above other trainers. We are all co-workers, trainers for Christ in the work of his Kingdom. What should you be looking for in these future Big Trainers? What are their characteristics?

### LOYAL, KIND AND KNOWLEDGEABLE SERVANTS
The Lord requests the following from his servants, and of course we should first and foremost, strive to attain this level ourselves: to pray, to be humble, to obey, to subjugate our bodies, to be faithful, and to learn from our role model, the Lord Jesus Christ, to be filled with love and blessings.

## PRAYER

Jesus prayed for a whole night before selecting his disciples (Luke 6:12). Similarly, we must pray respectfully and devoutly to seek God's will. Prayer is the best method to communicate, dialogue, and receive answers from God. If we rely on ourselves, we will not be able to find good co-workers; the only way is to listen to the Lord. At the same time, the co-worker we are looking for is one that is very focused on prayer and is a prayer warrior.

## HUMBLE

Humility is a very important quality in serving the Lord. Jesus was gentle and humble in heart. If we, as the Lord's servants, do not learn to be humble, how can we serve others? Jesus was humble enough to stoop and wash his disciple's feet. In the same way, we should also serve others with a similar attitude of humility. As we choose co-workers, we must also assess them from this angle.

## OBEDIENCE

Obeying the will of God is also a characteristic Jesus modeled for us to follow. As he obeyed our Heavenly Father's will, so we too must obey. How do we listen? How do we obey? Through prayer we receive his orders and through reading Scripture we obtain his instructions.

There is a saying in the army; "Obedience is the soldier's nature!"

Since we are the Lord's soldiers, should we not obey the Heavenly Father's will? His will is for us to adore him, love the lost, love all those around us and bless them so that they too may become children of God and disciples of Jesus.

## SUBJUGATE THE BODY

A good servant of the Lord is capable of self-control and would never indulge in his own desires. Keep control of yourself in everything and do everything for the glory of God. A person who is able to be responsible for himself will be able to be responsible for the work of the Lord.

The co-worker we need to search for needs to be one who seeks to continue to learn and improve, is always attentive to his work, and has a strong faith. Some may say this is too difficult or question how we can possibly find such an ideal co-worker. Yes, this may not be an easy task. Here are some guidelines for identifying and developing co-workers:

1. We must have faith that the Lord has prepared all over the world those who are after his heart. We need to seek God as he will guide us to them.

2. The gift God gives each person may be different. We need to find one who is effective and not one that is perfect. We need to help them stir up the gift God gave them so that they can be used by God.

3. This co-worker must trust you. He or she must have the same heart as you and accept your views and guidance. This is very important. Without the same heart, how can you walk together? Why would this person accept you? Is it simply because you can provide them what they need – Bible knowledge, a way of life, or a far and wide vision? If he respects you, and agrees with your teachings, he will naturally cooperate with you fully.

4. You need to take time to connect with potential co-workers. You can find co-workers by studying the Bible and praying together (in the beginning, start with at least half a day a week), sharing with them your spiritual experience and your plans, guiding them in how to answer God's calling and how to hear him, and training their hearts to be full of faith, love, patience, and godliness.

5. Lead by example with your training. Teach them: how to arrange a Mid-Level Retreat, how to plan the testimony and sharing meeting, how to pick various co-workers, etc.

6. They should be able to get in contact with you at any time (24/7), and discuss any problems they are facing.

## A PERSON OF CHRIST

Our goal is to train every believer to become a disciple of the Lord, so that each will become a person of Christ.

The person of Christ is often known as a "Christian." In fact, "Christian" should not just be a term we call ourselves. The first-time believers were called Christians was when the church in Antioch was established (Acts 11:26). The believers in the Antioch church had the Spirit of Jesus Christ in their hearts so that their every move had the likeness of Christ. Outsiders saw their actions as "small Christs," so they were called Christians (or persons of Christ).

I often think about the name, "Jesus Christ." Jesus is the Son of God. The name of Jesus is given to the world by the Heavenly Father, and only through this name can we be saved. Our sins can only be forgiven and we can only be saved if we accept, believe, and trust in the name of Jesus. None of us can truly be Jesus or be called Jesus. However, if we accept salvation from Jesus, we can be delivered from our sins. We must ask the Holy Spirit to live in our hearts so that we can become a living being with Jesus's Spirit within us. That is how we become a small Christ, a person of Christ, a Christian.

Praise the Lord, praise the Lord! You and I are both persons of Christ. Every trainer of the Lord is a disciple of the Lord. We must never forget that our aim is to train every disciple to become a "person of Christ!"

# 18

## Words of Encouragement

As you launch out in T4T, it may encourage you to know that you are not alone. Today thousands of men and women are using the simple principles of T4T to win Muslims, Hindus, Buddhists, and secularists into the Kingdom of God. As they train these new disciples they are rapidly expanding God's Kingdom around the world, reaching into every nation, tribe, and tongue with the good news of Christ's Kingdom.

## GETTING IT RIGHT

In my opinion, Ying and Grace, in listening and learning from the Holy Spirit's guidance, got it right.

I lived nearby Ying and Grace when he was working through the initial days of putting T4T together. We all were amazed to see the rapid and healthy multiplication as the Holy Spirit worked through new believers who were being taught to obey, even as Jesus commanded. We were asking questions of each other. "Can this really be happening? How long can this go forward?" And while asking, and doubting ourselves, and what we were seeing happen, we were encouraged repeatedly as we were testing, evaluating, and watching.

I continued going back to the Scriptures and saw this kind of movement in the New Testament record. Multiplication can be seen right after Pentecost, and in the work of Paul around Ephesus, and through other references in Scripture.

It has now been over 15 years since those early days, and I am gratified and thankful that T4T is being accepted in many places. The processes that Ying and Grace have modeled are proving to be effective across culture and geography

During those 15 plus years, we have learned many things that continue to bear fruit. We have learned that sometimes what is taught in the early stages of the training sessions can be modified to meet the needs of trainees in different parts of the world. We have also learned, and are still learning that whatever is taught, it should not be a knowledge 'dump', but training simple enough so that the new believer can grasp and replicate what has been taught.

We continue to see that the real test of 'success' is the trainee taking what he has learned, and training a fellow believer, perhaps someone he has led to faith. We have learned that Mid-Level Training is very important on a periodic basis. We have learned that checking and coaching 'down-stream' can help trainees become more fruitful as their trainer visits their groups, and gives personal encouragement and correction to the obedient trainee. We continue to see that training needs to continue not six, eight, or ten sessions, but needs to continue up to one year, and that is important to shift from the initial use of 'canned' Bible studies, to a more inductive style study of passages and books of the Bible.

Ying and Grace got it right. And what he shares here will help you. I trust you will find Ying's book to be encouraging and helpful in your ministry of multiplication, for our God loves fruit, and he loves and is glorified by much fruit, fruit that will last (John 15:2, 5, 8, and 16).

— Bill Fudge, Former Regional Leader, International
   Mission Board, SBC

## SOUTH ASIA

In 2003 I participated in a T4T training with Ying Kai. We had been involved in church planting in South Asia for the past 3-4 years and were failing forward. We had heard about disciples multiplying and churches multiplying, and we were beginning to see some of that in our own fields. God was moving, and I was under a leader who encouraged us to be learners of God's works.

So I sat and listened and got lots of reps practicing with Ying in the T4T training. Three things really struck me. One was Ying's reflection of the Father's heart. Ying had such a heart for the Father; it became so clear as he shared his heart and passion for the lost via some vision casting, it just flowed from his heart. I saw a man broken for lostness and driven by God's glory that all men would confess Christ.

Another lesson I learned came from an experience Ying had. Ying told us about a day he attempted to share the gospel with a man in the hospital, and the man told him to come back tomorrow. He respected the man's wishes and came back the next day. He went to the man's room to find that the man was not there. He asked the nurse where the man was. She shared that he had suddenly died that night. Ying was shocked! He said from then on, he would no longer ask permission to share the gospel, but instead he would share the gospel straight away.

Finally, there were many, many things Ying shared about vision that clearly reflected the Father's heart and passion and love for the people on earth who stand in judgment because of their fallen natures. As I listened to Ying, I heard his heart that he would ask, seek, and knock when he ran into obstacles. Whether learning a language so he could share the gospel, or needing God to open a new area, he would ask, seek, and knock to God the Father to see that the next city, the next factory, etc. could hear the gospel.

What I learned was how important it was to abide in Christ! The relationship with God will lead to an international outflow of gospeling and discipling. We began to attempt to find biblical vision casts we could share with leaders in Asia and help them develop patterns of the Father's heart.

I watched Ying train in the three-thirds pattern of care for discipleship. So I began trying to practice this in the discipleship of national brothers and also trying to train others in South Asia to do the same. As I watched the seven key parts of three-thirds, I realized this was a very simple process which allowed God to

sort out who and how to invest in disciples through the weekly accountability looking back at who had shared the gospel and who
had obeyed God's Word the past week. To me, it clearly challenged
people to the lordship of Christ, to obey what Christ commanded,
especially obeying the command to be a gospeling disciple.

There were new teachings each week from the Word of God.
You can't beat going through the Word of God verse-by-verse and
holding people accountable to obey the Word of God. Every week,
we would set goals to obey God's Word by sharing the gospel with
those far from God and by obeying Scripture to grow in Christ personally. You can't separate knowledge from obedience or obedience from the growing knowledge of God. They go hand-in-hand.
As new believers obey Christ's commands, they will grow in the
knowledge of Christ.

Three-thirds has become my pattern for Paul/Timothy relationships. It was so clear to me that Ying loved his leaders, and
he demonstrated this through his prayers and the time he gave
to them. I saw Ying train a third time during the SARS (Sudden
Acute Respiratory Syndrome) scare in East Asia. I saw him stop
training 50 folks so he could take a phone call to care for a leader
who was seeing friends and family die because of SARS. Ying was
so compassionate and loving, looked like what I saw in Scripture
of the love of the disciples of Christ.

We also developed a Mid-Level Retreat, a three-thirds meeting to care for the men and women of God, celebrating what God
had done in the past and giving new teachings from the Word
of God to receive future marching orders to obey. During these
times, we learned from one another what God was doing and to
take steps forward so that all may hear the gospel of Jesus Christ.
Character and integrity are what flow from these relationships
as folks are discipled.

Evidence of impact was soon visible in South Asia. Between
2006 and 2009, the 27 churches we'd started grew to 129 new
churches planted, more than 27,000 baptisms, and 786 T4T groups
connected to these new churches planted.

— Jeff Sundell, e3 Partners

## MUSLIM-FOCUSED T4T

I conducted an experiment with an old national, former-Muslim, church-planter friend. He had seen 200 baptisms and about a dozen churches started. He was seeing the typical fruit, but he was always at the center of it all: discipleship, evangelism, baptism, getting his people out of trouble, etc. We were not seeing churches planting churches.

I asked him to do an experiment with me. I asked him to:

1. Choose two churches and drop his attention from the other churches.

2. Let Brother Jay teach him T4T.

3. Try to plant 20 new churches in three months.

4. Instead of just doing the evangelism himself, he would train the new church members to do the evangelism.

5. He was to meet with his two churches three days each, every week and model for them how to do house church each time they met.

6. He was to pass on authority to every member of the two churches. That means that everyone would share the pastoral role, lead a participative Bible study, and practice baptism. I actually had them go back into the waters and practice baptism so that the church members would have no doubts that they had authority to baptize.

7. He also spent lots of time teaching Kevin Greeson's *Camel Method* [see Kevin Greeson, *The Camel, How Muslims Are Coming to Faith in Jesus Christ!* (Monument, CO: WIGTake Resources, 2011) for teaching them "what to say to a Muslim"].

8. He had the church members write out a list of who needed to hear the gospel. Then he challenged them to choose two from their list and go out and share. They had to report each time they met together.

The results were amazing. He reported to me in detail that in three months, they had started 14 new churches.

— A missionary in South Asia

## BANGLADESH

The Way of Peace Trust was founded in 2000 by a Bangladeshi believer we'll call Modi, and is dedicated to evangelism and church planting. Modi's vision is to share the love of Christ with his fellow Muslims in Bangladesh and in the world. Through the Way of Peace Trust, Modi is willing to do whatever it takes to fulfill the Great Commission through evangelism, making disciples, and sharing Christ's love with Bengali people in the world.

Modi reported: "Last March we had training in Mumbai with migrant Bengali folks. We trained 25 believers who were house church leaders, plus new believers. Following my training manual, we had T4T for three hours. I gave training, then I sent all the participants out two-by-two for outreach with new people. Then after two hours all of the brothers in Christ came back and gave their report. Eighty-six new folks received their savior the Lord Jesus Christ by prayer! We praise our great Lord Jesus Christ.

### Monthly Strategy- March-2016

| 1 | How many new people received water baptism | 70 |
|---|---|---|
| 2 | How many baptisms by new believers | 50 |
| 3 | How many Bibles received by new believers | 100 |
| 4 | How many tracts distributed to new people | 500 |
| 5 | How many first meetings with a person of peace | 1 |
| 6 | How many disciples in training | 4 |
| 7 | How many new house churches started | 3 |

    — A missionary in Bangladesh

## POLYNESIA

The T4T approach had never been tried in a Polynesian context. During the training, they sent several young men out on 'homework' assignments, sharing the gospel, and the first day 14 people accepted Christ.

"People started coming to Christ like crazy," Zack reported. In 2014, there were 275 who began to follow Jesus. Then 175 who accepted Christ went through the discipleship training and began to disciple others.

A young man named Carter, who works full-time at the bank, caught the vision and at one point was leading 17 groups. Carter began to train his girlfriend who was living in the capital of Nuku'alofa by phone.

Due to the overwhelming response, Zack and Anna decided to move to the capital and start T4T there. When he made contact with Carter's girlfriend, he discovered she was already leading six groups.

What is going on here? he wondered.

Zack met with the leaders of four denominations and they all wanted to go through the training. He is receiving invitations from Fiji, Tahiti, Samoa, and New Zealand to share about what he's seeing the Lord do on Tonga.

God has supplied a wave of the Spirit that goes beyond any surfing adventures he could have imagined. "It's like we're riding along and God is bringing the stuff and doing the stuff and we're not even doing it."

— Mark Ellis, Polynesia

## A MISSIONS REVOLUTION

In my opinion, T4T has done more to revolutionize the world of missions than anything else in the last 20 years. In my own ministry, I had very little clarity on how to really help develop leaders until learning the T4T process. Now, it is the cornerstone of everything I do as a missionary. God is using this process to develop the thousands of new church leaders He is raising up in South Asia. In one network alone, we went from six small churches to now more than 2,000 people per year coming to faith in Jesus.

We're literally seeing God multiply movements of church starts. We currently are seeing more than 50 of these streams across South Asia with each of them carrying the potential to impact millions of people. These national brothers and sisters have completely changed the way they disciple others from just delivering content to really helping transform the lives. Everyone is training their oikos to become trainers of others. T4T is simple but revolutionary. God is really using T4T principles in a very mighty way in South Asia.

— Chase Tozer, International Mission Board (SBC)
  Pseudonymized for security purposes

## TASMANIA

During our time of service in Tasmania, Australia, we began hearing about church-planting movements and wondered if such a thing could take place in a Western context. It seemed that most church leaders were looking for ways to help their churches grow, and occasionally giving emphasis to planting new churches, but I was intrigued by the idea that rapid movements could sweep through an entire nation.

In the meantime, I kept hearing many confusing voices about church, to a point where church seemed hopelessly complex. This made me all the more interested in how thousands of new churches were being formed by ordinary people—even new believers and uneducated people—in places like Asia.

In May 2006 I began eagerly seeking answers, and God was ready to teach me a lesson that would change my life forever. The Lord reminded me of the Great Commandment to love him and to love our neighbor. He also reminded me of the Great Commission to go and make disciples. Three phrases came into my mind during that time which served to remind me of these "three great commands," and from these I developed the acronym AIM: Accountability to One Another, Intimacy with God, and Multiplication of the Kingdom. Hearing this from the Lord was like drinking water in a desert.

Four months later, Judy and I were invited to attend Strategy Coordinator Training in Singapore. We studied with about 30 other workers from various parts of Asia and Europe to discuss scriptural mandates, disciple-making methods, and the methodology of church-planting movements. It was at this point that I met Ying and Grace Kai and learned about T4T for the first time.

I was amazed at both the effectiveness and simplicity of this method, but also humbled as God showed me clearly how T4T perfectly fit in my ministry that our Heavenly Father had taught me earlier that year.

I had no doubt that T4T was a God-inspired idea whose time had come—and I wanted to take it back to Australia. I wanted to know if it would possibly work in a place like Tasmania. I couldn't wait to get back and put it to work!

After several years of work and many mistakes, we maintained confidence that the seeds that were sown would one day produce much fruit. That happened as we began to see rapid multiplication in various directions. By 2013, we counted over 110 groups and churches in seven nations — all stemming from our meager work in remote Tasmania. We praise the Lord that he alone gives the increase. God can do it!

— Ben and Judy Armacost, Tasmania

## TOKYO

Our team is implementing T4T in the Tokyo area and passing on the principles to others in different regions of Japan. Almost every week we have reports of believers sharing the gospel for the first time, new training groups or outreach Bible studies being formed, salvations, and baptisms. We have also seen new churches emerging through the fruit.

We are still learning how to best adjust T4T to the Japanese context, but we are seeing much fruit through utilizing these New Testament principles of multiplication.

— David Cervenka, Tokyo

## SOUTHEAST ASIA

"They are starting more churches and they don't even tell us about it until after they start them!" The brothers and sisters I had been discipling and training shared that with me almost in exasperation. They weren't sure if there was something wrong with the rapid, multi-generational growth of disciples and new churches we were seeing. Far from there being something wrong however, it was obvious what we were witnessing was the work of God and we were blessed to be able to join in that work.

I had been involved in planting numerous churches before that time but the growth of disciples and churches had been mostly incremental. What we were seeing now was something totally different as new believers began to immediately share the gospel with family and friends – as new discipleship groups cascaded into second, third and fourth-generation groups – as new churches were starting from those discipleship groups multiplying throughout our city and to cities beyond.

Believers were taking the gospel to family and friends, to neighbors, to work, or on trips to other cities visiting friends, or on return trips to their hometown. As they carried the gospel with them they would lead people to Christ, disciple them and help them be the body of Christ in that place. And as that happened, the work multiplied and grew beyond our capability to track or keep up with. Praise God for this mighty wave of his Spirit at work.

The channel of God's blessing in this work was Training for Trainers (T4T). As I arrived and began working in East Asia, I heard many testimonies of God at work through Ying and Grace and I received some training in T4T. It was my prayerful desire to see a similar response to the gospel in the city where I was called.

The more I studied and began to apply T4T, the more I came to understand the important biblical principles upon which it is based. God desires us to be in an intimate, faith-filled, obedient relationship with him. The Father's heart is that all people might repent and return to him. My calling is that every believer is to go to the lost and not wait for them, to make them into Christ's disciples, to train them in the things that God has taught me and to stick with them to insure they are being obedient, to be accountable together with them. And in all of that Jesus has given his promise to be with me.

I learned that T4T was much more than a set of lessons or another program to follow. T4T is a biblical paradigm of an obedient discipleship relationship with God. That relationship with God in turn draws us into a prayer-fueled, mutually accountable relationship with other brothers and sisters in Christ. So it was together with what started as a small group of believers, we encouraged and challenged each other in our relationship with God, in our prayer life, in our devotional life. Through T4T, we practiced sharing our testimony with one another and then went out and shared it with the lost.

God took that small band of believers and turned them first into a handful of new churches. From a handful of new churches they continued to apply those same principles starting more churches until there were hundreds of new churches that continued to multiply this same faithful discipleship relationship with God.

God has now called us from that city in East Asia to another city in Southeast Asia. That previous work is still continuing, as the believers from those multiplying churches remain focused on winning the lost, discipling believers and starting churches. In this new city I have without hesitation once again started with the application of T4T in our work. It's been awesome to see already the beginnings of God working in the lives of new believers as they faithfully pass on what they are learning to others. God still loves the people of this world and it is still his will for us to make disciples of all peoples. Having received his grace, let us not have received it in vain.

— Adam Johnson, International Mission Board
Pseudonymized for security purposes

## ASSESSING T4T

What a joy it was to travel in East Asia with Ying Kai and his lovely wife Grace and see, meet, and interview generations of church leaders in multiple locations. As the Director of the Global Research Department of the Southern Baptist International Mission Board (IMB), I've had the privilege to conduct Church Planting Movement (CPM) assessments in many places, and never have I seen and heard stories of prayer, obedience, and sacrifice as I did in the largest CPM ever assessed by the IMB.

With three and a half years of monthly reports in hand before planning the assessment, we eagerly conducted interviews in tea shops, restaurants, markets, hotels, and assorted segments of one very large people group. In more than one place, we verified up to eight generations of believers in a single interview room.

We heard testimonies and witnessed T4T – inductive Bible studies, obedience-based discipleship, training of trainers. We traveled along roads and saw "training centers" – just houses that trainers use to train trainers with the training houses themselves multiplying as needed! While one can never assess all the places a movement has spread, we were allowed unhindered interview time with network trainers, pastors, and believers.

In one instance, a stranger tried to train Ying Kai himself, not knowing who he was. Finally, while the universals of CPMs were clearly evident in the movement we assessed, what was most remarkable to the team and to me was the evidence of holiness in the life of Ying Kai and Grace and the transformation of all they touched.

I was in the churches; I was with the trainers, and I was there in times of triumphant praise and victorious prayer. It is not a surprise to find God moving in ways beyond our comprehension—that's the kind of God we serve.

— Dr. Jim Haney, Director of Global Research,
   International Mission Board, SBC

## WORDS OF ENCOURAGEMENT FROM YING AND GRACE

These words from Ying and Grace have echoed across T4T trainings around the world and been translated into scores of languages. Though simple, they bear repeating:

**Pray!**

**Keep it simple!**

**Don't doubt that you can do it – just do it!**

**Be strong and courageous!**

**Do your work!**

**Your Heavenly Father will be with you!**

# APPENDIX A

## T4T Training Lessons

# Lesson 1
## *The Assurance of Salvation*

Congratulations, you are a child of the Heavenly Father (Acts 17:28-29)! From this point on, you can come into a new relationship with God and receive all of his promises.

## I. REVIEW HOW WE RECEIVE ETERNAL LIFE THROUGH JESUS.

A. What is the result of sin (Isaiah 59:2)? _____

_____

_____

B. People try many different ways to find God, yet fail. Why (Ephesians 2:8-9)? _____

_____

_____

C. How does God draw us to himself (1 Peter 3:18)? _____

_____

_____

## II. THE WAY OF SALVATION

A. The redemption of Jesus + your faith + repentance = salvation.

Has God done what he wants to do (death and resurrection)? _____ Yes _____ No

Have you done what you need to do (believe and repent)? _____ Yes _____ No

**If you have believed, then you are saved!**

B. What does Jesus promise to those who follow him (John 10:28)? _____

_____

C. Eternal life does not only mean you will live forever; life with God also means that we are able to live a life of holiness, righteousness, kindness, and strength. We will forever receive the blessings of God!

D. Believing in Christ not only means you will have eternal life, but starting right now, you have a new life, letting you feel peace, happiness, and blessings at this very moment. You will also become one to bless others.

## III. YOUR RESPONSE

Do you know you have been saved? _____ Yes _____ No

Do you know you have received eternal life? _____ Yes _____ No

**Conclusion:** _____ I have been saved. _____ I have not been saved. _____ I still don't know.

## IV. IF ANYONE IS IN CHRIST

If anyone is in Christ, he is a new _____, the _____ has gone, the _____ has come (2 Corinthians 5:17).

The saved will be changed. Have you experienced any of the following changes?

____ inner peace

____ awareness of sin

____ constantly feel God's love

____ desire to read the Bible

____ peace of having been forgiven

____ ability to defeat sin

____ attitude of becoming better

____ caring for others

## V. IF YOU SIN AGAIN, ARE YOU STILL SAVED? (HEBREWS 6:4-8; 10:26)

(1 John 1:9) _____

_____

(1 John 1:6-7) _____

_____

## VI. JOYFULLY FILL IN YOUR SPIRITUAL BIRTH CERTIFICATE.

On _____ (day) _____ (month) _____ (year), I received Jesus into my life to be my Savior. He forgave my sin, became my Lord, and took control of my life. Now I have become a child of God and a new creation. I have begun a new life following Him.

Signature: _____

## VII. MEMORIZE THIS BIBLE VERSE.

"He who has the Son has life, he who does not have the Son, does not have life." 1 John 5:12.

## VIII. TELL FIVE PERSONS.

When you receive this great salvation, your life is full of joy and peace! The first thing that you should do is to share this good news. **Tell five people what you have heard and learned today. In addition, train these individuals to share and train others.** In the following weeks, continue to teach at least five more individuals weekly. This is the great news and it is God's will; He is willing for all to receive salvation.

# Lesson 2
## Understanding Prayer

Every baby needs a new life, so he needs assurance of salvation. That was Lesson 1 (and 1B). When a baby has just been born, he or she needs to breathe. This lesson on prayer will teach you how to breathe in your new spiritual life.

Praying is talking with God. When you pray, you should be frank and sincere, the same way the Bible tells us that Jesus talked with God and taught his disciples.

## I. WHY DO WE NEED TO PRAY?

A. It is God's command:

"You should _____ pray." (Luke 18:1)

"And pray in the Spirit, _____." (Ephesians 6:18)

B. It is your need to seek God's leading:

"Cast all your _____ on him because _____" (1 Peter 5:7).

"If you _____ upon Me, I will show you _____ which you _____" (Jeremiah 33:3).

C. Receive mercy and find grace in your time of need (Hebrews 4:16).

How should we approach God's throne of grace? _____
_____

What will we receive and find? _____
_____

D. What things do you need to pray for?

"Do not be anxious about anything, but in _____ by prayer and petition, with thanksgiving, present your _____ to God. And the peace of God, which transcends all understanding, will guard your hearts and your minds in Christ Jesus" (Phil. 4:6-7).

## II.  THREE ANSWERS TO PRAYER

Yes -   Green Light: You can proceed.

No -   Red Light: You cannot proceed.

Wait -  Yellow Light: God does not respond, so you must be patient.

## III.  THE CONTENT OF PRAYER: DRAW A LINE BETWEEN THE VERSE AND THE CORRECT DESCRIPTION OF PRAYER.

Praise: praise God's nature                      1 John 1:9

Thanksgiving: thank God for his grace      Philippians 4:6-7

Ask: ask God to meet your own needs         Psalm 135:3

Intercession: ask God to meet the      1 Thessalonians 5:19
    needs of others

Confession: confess your sins to God          1 Timothy 2:1

## IV.  THE THREE-FOLD WILL OF GOD

A. What God has commanded us to do. This is what God has already determined; it can never be changed by what or how a person prays (e.g. love your neighbor as yourself).

B. What God allows. Sometimes if we plead with God, He will allow us to receive something, but we should be responsible for what we receive (not God's ideal for us).

C. What is pleasing to God (Romans 12:2).

# V. NEW ATTITUDES RESULTING FROM PRAYER

| ATTITUDE | VERSE |
|---|---|
| Have faith | "But when he asks, he must believe and not doubt." (James 1:6). |
| Have the right motivation | "You do not have, because you do not ask God. When you ask, you do not receive because you ask with the wrong motives (James 4:2-3). |
| Confess our sins | "If I cherish sin in my heart, the Lord would not have listened" (Psalm 66:18). |
| Ask according to his will | "This is the confidence we have in approaching God: that if we ask anything according to his will, he hears us" (1 John 5:14). |
| Pray with a faithful heart | "They should always pray and not give up" (Luke 18:1). |

# VI. HINTS FOR EFFECTIVE PRAYER

A. Pray "in Jesus's name" (John 14:13) because we can only come before God through Jesus (John 14:6).

B. Ending our prayer by saying "Amen" means praying with one's true heart and agreeing with what has been said. (1 Chronicles 16:36)

C. Prayer has many parts: praise, thanksgiving, requests, intercession, and confession. We should not favor any part and neglect the others.

D. Pray in a natural and understandable manner; avoid babbling.

E. Pray at any time of the day and at any place. There is no limit on the time and place of prayer.

# Lesson 3
## Daily Devotions

Now that the new spiritual baby has breath, it also needs to eat. Lesson three teaches us how to read the Bible and worship God by ourselves daily. To know a person, you need to have regular contact with him or her. Along those same lines, if you want to have a close relationship with God, you need to "set a time" just for God every day. We want to set a time for a daily devotional.

### I. THE CONTENT OF OUR DEVOTIONAL TIME
A. Talk with God through prayer

B. Let God speak to me through reading the Bible

### II. THE PURPOSE OF OUR DEVOTIONAL TIME
A. To worship God – God welcomes me

B. To fellowship with God – we share our concerns

C. To be led by God – I welcome God in my life

### III. THE ATTITUDE OF OUR DEVOTIONAL TIME
What attitude does the psalmist have toward God?

(Psalms 42:1-2) _____

_____

(Psalms 119:147-148) _____

_____

### IV. EXAMPLES FROM THE BIBLE
See chart on page 182.

From the examples below, what applications to your life can you make in terms of spending time with God? _____

_____

_____

## How did these people from the Bible seek and know God?

| VERSE | PERSON | TIME | PLACE | ACTIVITY |
|---|---|---|---|---|
| Genesis 19:27 | Abraham | Morning | | Met God |
| Psalms 5:3 | | | | |
| Daniel 6:10 | | | | |
| Mark 1:35 | | | | |

## V.   SUGGESTIONS AND TOOLS FOR YOUR SPIRITUAL LIFE

A. **Bible**: Write down the Scripture reference, read it, and write what you learned from the reading. Meditate on the verse. Remember that you can't change what the Bible says, but you can change how it impacts your life. There are many good devotional books, but none can replace the Bible. The Bible is the answer to humanity's four big questions. Where do I come from? Why do I exist? How should I live? Where will I go in the future?

B. **Pen and Notebook**: During your devotional time, write down your thoughts and what you sense God saying to you. "And you shall remember all the ways which the Lord your God has led you..." (Deut. 8:2). You can also write down the names and needs of those you are praying for. Also note answers to these prayers to encourage yourself.

C. **Place**: Choose a place where you can meet with God without being disturbed. God wants you to concentrate when facing Him.

D. **Time**: Find the most appropriate time where you can consistently meet with God.

E. **Plan**: Choose a Bible book to read at your own rate, and then meditate, record, pray, and obey.

## VI.   GETTING READY TO MEET WITH GOD – YOUR DEVOTIONAL PLAN

A. **Pray**: "Open my eyes that I may see wonderful things in your law." (Psalms 119:18)

B. **Prepare**: Collect the things you need and find a quite place. Prepare your heart and wait on God. Confess your sins.

C. **Seek God**: Read a Scripture portion. Meditate on how it relates to you. Talk with God about what you read. Pray over each item listed above.

D. **Follow Through**: Obey what God reveals to you. Share with others what you have learned.

E. Additional reading: Take time in other times in the day (now or before bed) to read larger amounts of Scripture. Begin reading three chapters from the Old Testament and one chapter from the New Testament each day. By doing this, you can read the whole Bible in about a year.

## VII. BE FAITHFUL TO KEEP YOUR DEVOTIONAL LIFE

Persevere in keeping your daily devotions; make the time a part of your daily life.

A. It is your decision to meet with God daily. If you keep a daily devotional time with God, you will grow in your spiritual life.

B. While Jesus was on earth, He said, "But seek first his Kingdom and his righteousness" (Matthew 6:33). In everything you might encounter in this world, nothing is more important than being with God.

C. One of God's desires is for you to have fellowship with him and to know him. Your goal should be to praise and worship God. Although devotions will bring you many good feelings, new insights, and many blessings, the main purpose of devotions is to know and worship God.

## YOUR COMMITMENT

Are you willing to commit to a daily devotion? ____ Yes ____ No

Signature_____

• Beginning date: _____

• Time or Times of Day: _____

• Place: _____

Below, describe your daily devotional plan. What books will you read? How will you pray? _____

_____

_____

_____

# Lesson 4
## The Church Gathering

When you become a Christian, you are a member of God's family. Every spiritual child needs to become a part of a spiritual family. God is your Heavenly Father, and all Christians are like brothers and sisters of the same family. "This household is the church of the living God..." (1 Timothy 3:15). The household is not a building, and the "church" is not a place of worship, but a group of believers.

## I. HOW DOES THE BIBLE DESCRIBE THE RELATIONSHIP BETWEEN JESUS AND CHRISTIANS?

(Romans 12:5) _____

_____

(Ephesians 1:22-23) _____

_____

## II. WHAT IS CHRIST'S POSITION IN THE CHURCH?

(Ephesians 5:23) _____

_____

## III. THE FUNCTIONS OF THE CHURCH

| FUNCTIONS | VERSE | YOUR NEEDS |
|-----------|-------|------------|
| Worship | "Praise God, sing to the Lord a new song, his praise in the assembly of the saints." (Psalms 149:1) | to worship God |
| Fellowship | "And let us consider how we can spur one another on toward love and good deeds." (Hebrews 10:24) | to share |

| Teaching | "…and teaching them to obey everything I have commanded you." (Matthew 28:20) | to learn to obey |
| Ministry | "…to prepare God's people for works of service so that the body of Christ may be built up." (Ephesians 4:12) | to serve |
| The Power of the Holy Spirit | "But you will receive power when the Holy Spirit has come upon you…" (Acts 1:8) | to spread the gospel |

## IV.  CAN CHRISTIANS TODAY NOT ATTEND CHURCH?

___ Yes ___ No ___ It Depends

Do you have difficulty attending church? ___ Yes ___ No ___ It Depends

## V.  WHY SHOULD YOU ATTEND CHURCH?

A. Because we need worship, fellowship, teaching, ministry and the Holy Spirit's power.

B. Because this is God's command. "And let us not _____ our meeting together, as some people do, but _____ and _____ each other, especially now that the day of his _____ again is drawing near" (Hebrews 10:25).

C. To avoid deviating from the truth of the Bible.

D. Because there are mature Christians in church to help you.

## VI.  THREE OBLIGATIONS WE HAVE IN CHURCH

A. Our obligation to be united with Christ – Baptism (Romans 6:1-14)

1) Baptism is a fulfillment of our faith.

- Jesus said that baptism was to "fulfill all righteousness" (Matthew 3:15).

- Jesus set an example for us. He was baptized even though He never sinned, but because He knew it was the right thing to do.

2) Baptism is a proclamation of our faith.

- The words and actions of baptism communicate to those present that we are positioned in Christ Jesus (Romans 6:3).

3) Baptism is a confirmation of our faith.

- We know and feel that we are freed from the old dead person, and live a new life of resurrection power (Romans 6:6-14).

4) Baptism is a witness of our faith.

- Baptism is to show that we are dead, buried and resurrected together with the Lord.

   *We were therefore _____ with him through baptism into _____ in order that, just as Christ was _____ from the dead through the _____ of the Father, we too may live a _____ life"* (Romans 6:4).

5) Baptism is a symbol of our faith.

- Baptism does not have the power to forgive sins. We are saved when we confess with our mouth and believe in our heart (Romans 10:9).

B. Our obligation to remember – The Lord's Supper

1) Jesus personally set the Lord's Supper as a remembrance of his death and shedding of blood for our sins. (Matthew 26:17-19, 26-30)

2) When we take the Lord's Supper, it helps us to remember and to give thanks.

   "The _____ that brought us _____ was upon him, and by _____ we are _____" (Isaiah 53:5).

3) When we receive the Lord's Supper, we have time to examine our actions and faith (1 Corinthians 11:23-29).

C. Our obligation to give – Offerings

Offerings are thank-you gifts given to God as acts of worship. Offerings can include sacrifices of a person's life, time, and finances. Monetary offerings are required by God and are a test of the disciple's faith, love, and obedience. Three kinds of monetary offerings are mentioned in the Bible.

1) Tithes. God commands us to tithe; the tithe belongs to God. It is not a voluntary offering, but what we are required to give (Leviticus 27:30–31). The tithe should be paid; you can decide what to do with the other 90%, but we should give 10% back to God because it already belongs to him.

   *"Will a mere _____ rob God? Yet you rob me. But you ask, 'How are we robbing you?' In _____ and _____. You are under a curse, your whole _____, because you are robbing me. Bring the whole _____ into the storehouse, that there may be food in my house. _____ me in this," says the Lord Almighty, "and see if I will not throw open the floodgates of _____ and pour out so much _____ that there will not be room enough to _____ it"* (Malachi 3:8-10).

2) Gifts and Offerings. This is a truly voluntary offering arising from a thankful and sincere heart. The amount of the gift is your own personal decision. We cannot worship God without gifts and offerings. We should not continually come empty-handed into God's presence.

3) Love Offerings. This is offering given to others. It is motivated by love and is given according to what a person has and according to the needs of others. Gift and love offerings cannot replace the tithe.

This week, make a commitment to becoming a church together. Begin adding these three obligations into your meeting times.

# Lesson 5
## God Is Our Heavenly Father

When a spiritual baby is born, he has new life. He knows how to breathe, how to eat, and how to have a family life. But now he needs to know who is in charge of the family: Our Heavenly Father. Jesus taught his disciples to say, "Our Father who art in heaven." The Heavenly Father loves, protects, provides for, and disciplines (trains) his children.

## I. THE HEAVENLY FATHER'S LOVE

*"The Lord appeared to them from afar saying, 'I have _____ you with an everlasting _____,' therefore I have drawn you with lovingkindness."* (Jeremiah 31:3)

A. Why did God save you?

_____ because you are so bad?

_____ because you first loved him?

_____ because you have bad luck?

_____ because _____

*"But because of his great _____ for us, God, who is rich in mercy, made us alive with Christ even when we were _____ in _____—it is by _____ you have been saved."* (Ephesians 2:4-5).

B. How does God reveal his love to you? Please write an example below. _____

_____

(1 John 3:1) _____

_____

C. In Luke 15:11-24, Jesus talks about how a father loved a son. What are the similarities between this father and God our Father? _____

_____

_____

## II.  THE HEAVENLY FATHER'S PROTECTION

*"But the Lord is faithful, and he will_____*
*you from the evil one."* (2 Thessalonians 3:3).

A. In Psalm 34:7, what does God promise? _____

_____

B. How did God protect Elijah (2 Kings 6:15-18)? _____

_____

C. How did God protect the three friends (Daniel 3)? _____

_____

D. How does God protect you when you face temptation? _

_____

(1 Corinthians 10:13) _____

_____

## III.  THE HEAVENLY FATHER'S PROVISION

*"And my God will _____ all your _____ accord-*
*ing to his glorious _____ in Christ Jesus"* (Philippians
4:19).

A. Why are God's children not to worry?

(Matthew 6:31-32) _____

_____

B. What gift has God given his children to demonstrate he
is willing to meet our needs?

(Romans 8:32) _____

_____

## IV.  GOD'S DISCIPLINE

*"Because the Lord _____ those He loves, and He*
*_____ everyone He accepts as a_____"* (Hebrews
12:6).

A. What does God expect for his children?

(Ephesians 4:13) _____

_____

B. How does God discipline his children?

    1)  Through friends (Proverbs 27:17) _____

    _____

    2)  Through the Bible (2 Timothy 3:16) _____

    _____

    3)  Through trials (James 1:2-4) _____

    _____

## V. WHICH ASPECT OF GOD IS MOST MEANINGFUL TO YOU?

___ his love and kindness

___ his provision for your needs

___ his discipline

___ his protection

# Lesson 6
## Spreading the Gospel

You are now a Christian, a child of God, a member of God's family. You have assurance of salvation. You can pray directly to God and have fellowship with him at any time and spend devotional time with him. You are a member of his church, a blessed people. Now that you are maturing, you need to give back to the family. God calls you to spread the gospel and teach new believers to obey all of his ways. Then they can proceed to teach even more people about the good news of salvation and train them also.

There are four types of calls to share the gospel that we should hear each day.

## I. CALL FROM ABOVE – FROM HEAVEN
The commandment of the Lord Jesus. (Isaiah 6:1-8 – The Lord calling for someone to go)

(Mark 16:15) _____

_____

The Lord commands us to go. That is enough. Point your finger upward. This call comes from above, from heaven.

## II. CALL FROM BELOW – FROM HELL
The rich man's plea for someone to share the gospel with his family.

(Luke 16:27-28) _____

_____

_____

The lost in hell call us to go warn their family members who are still alive. Can you hear them? Point your finger downward. This call comes from below, from hell.

## III.  CALL FROM THE INSIDE

Paul was under compulsion to spread the gospel.

(1 Corinthians 9:16-17) _____

_____

A voice inside us tells us that we were created to be witnesses. Can you hear it? Point your finger at your heart. This call comes from inside, from our hearts.

## IV.  CALL FROM THE OUTSIDE

Paul heard the call from a lost man in Macedonia to come help.

(Acts 16:9) _____

_____

Outside voices from lost people all around us are calling us to help them. With their mouths, they may say nothing, but their hearts call for us to share the good news with them. Can you hear them? Point your finger outside. This call comes from outside, from the lost around us.

Today every Christian should listen to the calls in their life and respond immediately. Point your finger up, down, in, and out several times and repeat the four calls.

- We should not only lead people to become Christians, but also to become successful trainers, training others to do share the gospel too. In this way, you can rapidly spread the gospel message.

  (2 Timothy 2:2) _____

  _____

- God's desire is for every Christian to start at least one new group, sharing the gospel with his family and friends. God will greatly bless and use his life.

  (Acts 2:46-47) _____

  _____

- You should immediately respond to God and pray for the body of Christ. Ask God to help you be a blessing by doing these things:

1) Leading people to faith in the Lord

2) Starting at least one new church or home group (at your own home or any place)

3) Training trainers (people who will repeat the process and train their new trainers)

# Lesson 7
## *Participatory Bible Study*

From this point on, when you meet as a group, you will simply open the Bible and study it together, asking God to show you what to obey and pass on to others. As you individually and as a group have the Holy Spirit in your heart, know that he will serve as your teacher and help you to understand and obey God's Word. Using a similar pattern each week makes it easy to dig out the truth of the Bible no matter what passage you are studying.

## THE PATTERN
Read the pattern that Ezra, a teacher of the Bible, used in Ezra 7:10. What are the three things that Ezra did?

1. _____

2. _____

3. _____

Essentially, Ezra tried to answer three questions – S.O.S.!

1. What does this passage SAY?

2. What should I do to OBEY it?

3. What should I teach or SHARE with others?

Every time you study the Word, you should try to answer these three questions.

## THE POWER
You have the ability to understand the Bible because of the Helper that God has sent to live in your life – the Holy Spirit. How does he help you?

(John 14:26) _____

_____

(1 John 2:27) _____

_____

Before you begin studying the Bible on your own or as a group, always ask the Holy Spirit to fill you and guide you into understanding the truth of the Bible and give you the ability to obey it.

## A WEEKLY PLAN
It is helpful to study a book of the Bible passage by passage from the beginning to end over the course of several weeks or months. Or you can study a series of Bible stories. One example is given at the end of this lesson. Each week, use the S.O.S. pattern to study the Bible.

How do you understand what the Bible passage you are reading says? What does it mean? Here is a guide on how to start.

- **READ** a passage of Scripture (usually between a paragraph and a chapter) out loud in the group. If it is not too long, read it two to three times.

- **PRAY**: Ask for the Spirit to guide you to understand and obey it.

## I. WHAT DOES THIS PASSAGE SAY?
Ask these additional questions to help you understand the Bible.

- What is the main message? (Don't spend the majority of time on minor issues.)

- Make sure every answer comes from the Bible, not your own ideas or opinions.

## II. WHAT SHOULD I OBEY?
- Try to focus on very practical ways you can obey and apply what the Bible says. Is there a command to obey, an example to follow, or a promise to hold onto?

- Never study the Bible without asking God how to obey it. Otherwise, you will have a lot of knowledge without a changed life. Make a commitment to obey these things and ask each other about them.

## III. WHAT SHOULD I SHARE WITH OTHERS?

- Think about others who need to hear something you heard today.

- Make a plan to share this with them this week.

When you are done studying the Bible, pray. Ask God to give you the courage to obey this week and to share with others. Thank him for speaking to you.

# APPENDIX B

## T4T Basic Bible Studies

# Basic Bible Study Plan

After the first seven T4T lessons, you can use the following passages as a plan for the Participatory Bible Study time. You can do more than one passage at a time if you like.

## MARK BIBLE STUDY COURSE MATERIAL

1. Mark 1:1-8
2. Mark 1:9-15
3. Mark 1:16-20
4. Mark 1:21-28
5. Mark 1:29-34
6. Mark 1:35-45
7. Mark 2:1-12
8. Mark 2:13-17
9. Mark 2:18-28
10. Mark 3:1-12
11. Mark 3:13-19
12. Mark 3:20-30
13. Mark 3:31-35
14. Mark 4:1-20
15. Mark 4:21-25
16. Mark 4:26-29
17. Mark 4:30-34
18. Mark 4:35-41
19. Mark 5:1-20
20. Mark 5:21-24; 35-43
21. Mark 5:25-34
22. Mark 6:1-6
23. Mark 6:7-13
24. Mark 6:14-29
25. Mark 6:30-32
26. Mark 6:33-44
27. Mark 6:45-52
28. Mark 6:53-56
29. Mark 7:1-13
30. Mark 7:14-23
31. Mark 7:24-30
32. Mark 7:31-37
33. Mark 8:1-10
34. Mark 8:11-21
35. Mark 8:22-26
36. Mark 8:27-38; 9:30-32
37. Mark 9:1-8
38. Mark 9:9-13
39. Mark 9:14-29
40. Mark 9:30-32
41. Mark 9:33-37
42. Mark 9:38-50
43. Mark 10:1-12
44. Mark 10:13-16
45. Mark 10:17-31
46. Mark 10:32-34
47. Mark 10:35-45
48. Mark 10:46-52
49. Mark 11:1-11
50. Mark 11:12-18
51. Mark 11:19-26
52. Mark 11:27-33
53. Mark 12:1-12
54. Mark 12:13-17
55. Mark 12:18-27
56. Mark 12:28-34
57. Mark 12:35-40
58. Mark 12:41-44
59. Mark 13:1-8
60. Mark 13:9-13
61. Mark 13:14-27
62. Mark 13:28-37

63. Mark 14:1-10
64. Mark 14:11-21
65. Mark 14:22-26
66. Mark 14:27-31
67. Mark 14:32-42
68. Mark 14:43-52
69. Mark 14:53-65

70. Mark 14:66-72
71. Mark 15:1-15
72. Mark 15:16-47
73. Mark 16:1-8
74. Mark 16:9-13
75. Mark 16:14-20

## ACTS BIBLE STUDY COURSE MATERIAL

1. 1:1-11
2. 1:12-26
3. 2:1-13
4. 2:14-36
5. 2:37-42
6. 2:43-47
7. 3:1-10
8. 3:11-26
9. 4:1-22
10. 4:23-31
11. 4:32-37
12. 5:1-11
13. 5:12-16
14. 5:16-42
15. 6:1-7
16. 6:8-15
17. 7:1-53
18. 7:54-60
19. 8:1-8
20. 8:9-25
21. 8:26-40
22. 9:1-9
23. 9:10-19
24. 9:20-31
25. 9:32-35
26. 9:36-43
27. 10:1-23
28. 10:24-33
29. 10:34-48
30. 11:1-18
31. 11:19-30

32. 12:1-19
33. 12:20-24
34. 13:1-3
35. 13:4-12
36. 13:13-41
37. 13:42-52
38. 14:1-7
39. 14:8-20
40. 14:21-28
41. 15:1-21
42. 15:22-35
43. 15:35-41
44. 16:1-5 45. 16:6-10
46. 16:11-15
47. 16:16-40
48. 17:1-9 49.
49. 17:10-34
50. 18:1-17
51. 18:18-28
52. 19:1-10
53. 19:11-20
54. 19:21-41
55. 20:1-6
56. 20:7-12
57. 20:13-38
58. 21:1-16
59. 21:17-26
60. 21:27-40
61. 22:1-21
62. 22:22-30
63. 23:1-11

64. 23:12-35
65. 24:1-9
66. 24:10-23
67. 24:24-27
68. 25:1-12
69. 25:13-27
70. 26:1-11
71. 26:12-18
72. 26:19-23
73. 25:23-32
74. 26:1-11

75. 26:12-18
76. 26:19-32
77. 27:1-12
78. 27:13-26
79. 27:27-38
80. 27:39-44
81. 28:1-6
82. 28:7-10
83. 28: 11-16
84. 28: 17-22
85. 28: 23-31

## I TIMOTHY BIBLE STUDY COURSE MATERIAL

1. 1:1-11
2. 1:12-20
3. 2:1-7
4. 2:8-15
5. 3:1-7
6. 3:8-16
7. 4:1-5
8. 4:6-10
9. 4:11-16

10. 5:1-16
11. 5:17-21
12. 5:22-25
13. 6:1-2
14. 6:3-5
15. 6:6-10
16. 6:11-16
17. 6:17-22

## II TIMOTHY BIBLE STUDY COURSE MATERIAL

1. 1:1-7
2. 1:8-12
3. 1:12-18
4. 2:1-7
5. 2:8-10
6. 2:12-13
7. 2:14-15
8. 2:16-18

9. 2:19-21
10. 2:22-26
11. 3:1-9
12. 3:10:17
13. 4:1-5
14. 4:6-8
15. 4:9-22

## TITUS BIBLE STUDY COURSE MATERIAL

1. 1:1-4
2. 1:5-9
3. 1:10-2:2

4. 2:3-10
5. 2:11-15
6. 3:1-15

After reading the above books, you can study other books of the Bible. Ephesians or Romans are often helpful at this point.

# About the Authors

With decades of experience in the pastorate and as missionaries with the Southern Baptist International Mission Board, Ying and Grace Kai currently serve as Executive Directors of T4T Global Missions. In T4T, the Kais have developed one of the most fruitful methods for church planting and disciple training in the world. Every year more than 20,000 believers around the world receive their T4T training and with it have experienced life transformation as disciples of Jesus Christ.

# Acknowledgments

We thank the Lord for his great love and the movement of the Holy Spirit, which has allowed us to publish this book. We would like to dedicate this book to all those with the mindset to follow Jesus's Great Commission – that "this gospel of the Kingdom will be preached in the whole world as a testimony to all nations" and "make disciples of all nations."

We would also like to take this time to thank the body of Christ for their encouragement and support. We would like to thank our sons, Samuel, Joshua, and especially Moses who translated the entire book, and John Mark Hansen who also contributed to the translation, and David Garrison for his help in editing of this book. We pray that the Lord blesses this book and all those who read it.